THE AUSTRALIAN
Women's Weekly
Greek cooking

acp
books

Contents

The oven temperatures in this book are for conventional ovens; if you have a fan-forced oven, decrease the temperature by 10-20 degrees.

Greek cooking

For the Greeks food is a ritual. It is an experience that is shared in the company of family and friends. It is about love, spirituality and philosophy and as one of the most ancient cuisines, its culinary traditions have been celebrated for thousands of years.

The Greeks' love affair with food is one of their richest cultural assets. Their food is a reflection of their warmth and generosity, and their hospitality is legendary. Greek food is fresh, seasonal, simple and incredibly nutritious. With 20 per cent of Greece made up of islands and no part of the mainland more than a few hundred kilometres from the sea, fish and seafood are a popular part of the Greek diet. In fact, Greece's geography and climate play a vital role in many of its recipe's main ingredients. The rocky terrain has meant that goats and sheep have thrived there and this is evident in traditional dishes such as lamb fillo pie, goat and capsicum stew and roasted lamb shoulder. There are also the gorgeous sheep's and goat's milk cheeses – most famously of course fetta, a key ingredient in the iconic greek salad. The climate is perfect for growing olive and lemon trees, producing two of the most important elements of Greek cooking.

Greeks generally dine late at night when the temperature has cooled down. They sit and eat mezze, drink spirits and wine and converse for hours with loved ones. The mezze is a romantic notion employed by the Greeks to not only complement and enhance the taste of the drink but to provide the backdrop for a social gathering. Mezze are little plates shared by everyone at the table and unlike appetisers are not intended to whet the appetite for the next meal, but to be experienced as a meal in themselves. The variety of a mezze spread is diverse and adaptable. With everything from cheese fillo triangles and pan-fried haloumi to prawn souvlakia and meatballs in tomato sauce, Greek mezze caters to everyone's personal preferences.

It is not surprising that a culture so focused on food, family and celebration holds great enthusiasm for big festivals and religious holidays. The most notable in the Greek calendar is undoubtedly Easter. It is a colourful and vibrant time where streets and homes are decorated with painted eggs, and food is at the centre of all festivities. They celebrate by inviting friends and family to visit and exchange best wishes, food, conversation, love and laughter – a common thread in every aspect of Greek entertaining.

This book is full of delicious traditional Greek fare and the recipes are celebrated and beloved by Greeks the world over. Share these dishes with your loved ones and adopt the Greek eating culture to evoke laughter, happiness and love in your kitchen. Be inspired by Greek hospitality and cherish the process at every stage of cooking, for this food is about more than just sustenance: it is a celebration of life.

mezze

eggplant dip

2 medium eggplants (600g)
¼ cup (60ml) olive oil
2 tablespoons finely chopped fresh
   flat-leaf parsley
½ small red onion (50g), chopped finely
1 medium ripe tomato (150g), chopped finely
1 tablespoon lemon juice

1 Stab eggplants all over with a fork. Grill eggplants over low flame of gas or barbecue until charred and tender. When eggplants are cool enough to handle, pull away and discard skin.
2 Coarsely chop eggplant flesh; combine with oil in large bowl. Stir in remaining ingredients; season to taste.

prep + cook time 25 minutes (+ cooling)
makes 2½ cups
nutritional count per tablespoon 1.9g total fat (0.3g saturated fat); 84kJ (20 cal); 0.6g carbohydrate; 0.3g protein; 0.5g fibre

note Grilling the eggplant over a flame gives it a smoky flavour. If you find it too messy, you can also roast them in the oven or in a covered barbecue.

serving suggestion Pitta bread.

roasted fennel dip

Preheat oven to 200°C/400°F. Halve 4 baby fennel bulbs (520g) with fronds lengthways; remove and discard cores. Reserve 2 teaspoons coarsely chopped fennel fronds. Combine fennel with 2 cloves unpeeled garlic and 1 tablespoon olive oil in small baking dish; roast, uncovered, about 30 minutes or until fennel is tender. Cool. Peel garlic; blend or process fennel and garlic with 1 cup (240g) sour cream until smooth. Serve dip sprinkled with reserved fennel fronds.

prep + cook time 45 minutes (+ cooling)
makes 1½ cups
nutritional count per tablespoon 6.4g total fat (3.6g saturated fat); 268kJ (64 cal); 0.8g carbohydrate; 0.4g protein; 0.4g fibre

artichoke spinach dip

Preheat oven to 200°C/400°F. Rinse and drain 340g (11 ounces) bottled marinated artichokes; chop artichokes coarsely. Combine artichokes with 250g (8 ounces) thawed frozen chopped spinach, ½ cup (120g) sour cream, ¼ cup (75g) mayonnaise, ¾ cup (60g) coarsely grated kefalotyri cheese and 1 clove crushed garlic in medium bowl. Transfer mixture to 2-cup (500ml) ovenproof dish; bake, covered, 20 minutes.

prep + cook time 30 minutes **makes** 2 cups
nutritional count per tablespoon 2.7g total fat (1.3g saturated fat); 130kJ (31 cal); 0.7g carbohydrate; 1.1g protein; 0.4g fibre

taramasalata

Boil, steam or microwave 1 large (300g) coarsely chopped potato until tender; cool. Refrigerate until cold. Mash potato in small bowl with 90g (3 ounces) tarama, ½ small (40g) finely grated white onion, ¾ cup (180ml) extra light olive oil, ¼ cup (60ml) white wine vinegar and 1 tablespoon lemon juice until smooth.

prep + cook time 25 minutes (+ refrigeration)
makes 1⅔ cups
nutritional count per tablespoon 10.7g total fat (1.6g saturated fat); 472kJ (113 cal); 2.6g carbohydrate; 1.6g protein; 0.3g fibre

notes Tarama is salt-cured carp or cod roe, available in fish shops.
This recipe uses mashed potato but there are variations using bread soaked in water.
The colour of this dip can vary from beige to pink depending on the roe (commercial taramasalata is often coloured pink).

tzatziki

Place 500g (1 pound) yogurt onto large square of double-thickness muslin. Tie ends of muslin together; hang over large bowl, or place in a sieve to drain. Refrigerate about 2 hours or until yogurt is thick; discard liquid in bowl. Meanwhile, combine 1 peeled and coarsely grated lebanese cucumber (130g) and ½ teaspoon salt in small bowl; stand 20 minutes. Gently squeeze excess liquid from cucumber. Combine yogurt and cucumber in small bowl with 1 clove crushed garlic, 1 tablespoon lemon juice and 2 tablespoons finely chopped fresh mint; season to taste.

prep + cook time 10 minutes (+ refrigeration)
makes 1¾ cups
nutritional count per tablespoon 1.7g total fat (1.1g saturated fat); 125kJ (30 cal); 2.3g carbohydrate; 1.4g protein; 0.1g fibre

notes Muslin, a cotton cloth, is available in craft and cookware shops.
There are many variations of this classic mezze: cucumber can be diced instead of grated, you can use dill and parsley instead of mint. It's a great side to most meat dishes.

fetta and spinach stuffed potato balls

450g (14½ ounces) sebago potatoes,
  chopped coarsely
180g (5½ ounces) spinach, trimmed,
  shredded finely
150g (4½ ounces) fetta cheese, crumbled
50g (1½ ounces) butter
⅔ cup (160ml) water
1 teaspoon salt
1 cup (150g) plain (all-purpose) flour
2 eggs
vegetable oil, for deep-frying

1 Boil, steam or microwave potato until tender; drain. Mash potato in large bowl; cover to keep warm.
2 Meanwhile, boil, steam or microwave spinach until just wilted; drain. When cool enough to handle, squeeze excess liquid from spinach. Combine in medium bowl with cheese.
3 Melt butter in medium saucepan, add the water and salt; bring to the boil. Remove from heat; immediately stir in flour. Using a wooden spoon, beat until mixture forms a smooth ball. Beat in eggs and potato until smooth.
4 Using floured hands, roll level tablespoons of dough into balls; use finger to press hole into centre of each ball. Fill holes with level teaspoons of spinach mixture; roll potato balls gently to enclose filling.
5 Heat oil in large saucepan; deep-fry balls, in batches, until browned lightly. Drain on absorbent paper.

prep + cook time 1 hour 10 minutes **makes** 30
nutritional count per ball 5.1g total fat (2g saturated fat); 293kJ (70 cal); 3.8g carbohydrate; 2.1g protein; 0.5g fibre

note You can also use lasoda or pink-eye potatoes for this recipe.

herbed fetta cheese

200g (6½ ounces) fetta cheese
30g (1 ounce) unsalted butter, softened
2 tablespoons finely chopped fresh oregano
1 tablespoon finely chopped fresh mint
1 teaspoon finely grated lemon rind
2 teaspoons olive oil

1 Grease 1¼-cup (310ml) dish; line with plastic wrap.
2 Process cheese and butter until smooth. Transfer to medium bowl; stir in herbs and rind. Season with pepper. Press mixture firmly into dish. Cover; refrigerate 2 hours.
3 Unmould cheese onto plate; drizzle with oil.

prep time 15 minutes (+ refrigeration)
makes 1¼ cups
nutritional count per teaspoon 1.3g total fat (0.8g saturated fat); 60kJ (14 cal); 0g carbohydrate; 0.6g protein; 0g fibre

note You can vary the herbs or add finely chopped olives, if you like.

serving suggestions Celery sticks and bread.

spinach and cheese parcels

500g (1 pound) bunch spinach, trimmed,
  chopped finely
1 cup (80g) coarsely grated kefalotyri cheese
1 cup (200g) cottage cheese
2 tablespoons finely chopped fresh mint
1 egg
12 sheets fillo pastry
2 tablespoons olive oil

1 Preheat oven to 220°C/425°F. Oil oven trays,
line with baking paper.
2 Cook spinach in large frying pan until wilted;
drain. When cool enough to handle, squeeze
excess moisture from spinach. Combine spinach in
medium bowl with cheeses, mint and egg; season.
3 Brush 1 sheet of pastry with oil; top with 3 more
sheets, brushing each with oil. Cut layered sheets
into quarters then cut quarters in half to make
8 rectangles. Place 1 tablespoon of cheese mixture
in centre of each rectangle. Fold in sides, leaving
centre open. Repeat to make a total of 24 parcels.
4 Place parcels on tray; brush with oil. Bake about
15 minutes or until browned lightly.

prep + cook time 45 minutes **makes** 24
nutritional count per parcel 3.3g total fat (1.2g
saturated fat); 260kJ (62 cal); 4.6g carbohydrate;
3.5g protein; 0.4g fibre

notes When working with the first four sheets of pastry,
cover remaining pastry with a sheet of baking paper
then a damp tea towel to prevent it drying out.
You can also make this recipe with silver beet; remove
the white stalks and veins first.

dolmades

2 tablespoons olive oil
2 medium brown onions (300g), chopped finely
155g (5 ounces) lean minced (ground) lamb
¾ cup (150g) white long-grain rice
2 tablespoons pine nuts
½ cup finely chopped fresh flat-leaf parsley
2 tablespoons each finely chopped
  fresh dill and mint
¼ cup (60ml) lemon juice
2 cups (500ml) water
500g (1 pound) preserved vine leaves
¾ cup (200g) yogurt

1 Heat oil in large saucepan; cook onion, stirring, until softened. Add lamb; cook, stirring, until browned. Stir in rice and pine nuts. Add herbs, 2 tablespoons of the juice and half the water; bring to the boil. Reduce heat; simmer, covered, 10 minutes or until water is absorbed and rice is partially cooked. Cool.
2 Rinse vine leaves in cold water. Drop leaves into a large saucepan of boiling water, in batches, for a few seconds, transfer to colander; rinse under cold water, drain well.
3 Place a vine leaf, smooth-side down on bench, trim large stem. Place a heaped teaspoon of rice mixture in centre. Fold stem end and sides over filling; roll up firmly. Line medium heavy-based saucepan with a few vine leaves; place rolls, close together, seam-side down, on leaves.
4 Pour over the remaining water; cover rolls with any remaining leaves. Place a plate on top of leaves to weigh down rolls. Cover pan tightly, bring to the boil. Reduce heat; simmer, over very low heat, 1½ hours. Remove from heat; stand, covered, about 2 hours or until liquid has been absorbed.
5 Serve dolmades with combined yogurt and remaining juice.

prep + cook time 3 hours (+ standing) **serves** 10
nutritional count per serving 7.6g total fat (1.6g saturated fat); 690kJ (165 cal); 14.9g carbohydrate; 7.7g protein; 3.2g fibre

fried chilli prawns with garlic and lemon yogurt

500g (1 pound) small uncooked prawns (shrimp)
1 cup (150g) plain (all-purpose) flour
1 teaspoon ground chilli
vegetable oil, for deep-frying

GARLIC AND LEMON YOGURT
¾ cup (210g) greek-style yogurt
1 clove garlic, crushed
1 teaspoon finely grated lemon rind
1 tablespoon lemon juice

1   Make garlic and lemon yogurt.
2   Heat vegetable oil in medium saucepan or wok.
Toss unshelled prawns in combined flour and chilli;
shake away excess. Deep-fry prawns, in batches,
until browned lightly. Drain on absorbent paper.
Season with salt and a little extra ground chilli to
taste. Serve with lemon wedges.
3   Serve prawns with yogurt.

GARLIC AND LEMON YOGURT Combine
ingredients in small bowl; season to taste.

prep + cook time 20 minutes **serves** 6 as a starter
nutritional count per serving 8.2g total fat (2.7g
saturated fat); 866kJ (207 cal); 12.9g carbohydrate;
20g protein; 0.7g fibre

skordalia

3 medium potatoes (600g), unpeeled
3 cloves garlic
½ teaspoon salt
½ cup (125ml) olive oil
¼ cup (60ml) lemon juice
½ cup (125ml) milk

1 Boil, steam or microwave potatoes until tender.
Drain.
2 Meanwhile, pound garlic and salt in a mortar
and pestle until smooth, or, chop the garlic and
salt together on a board and use the flat side of
the knife blade to press garlic into a paste.
3 When potatoes are cool enough to handle,
halve and spoon out flesh. Push flesh through
sieve into large bowl. Whisk in oil, juice and
garlic mixture then milk. Season with salt and
white pepper.

prep + cook time 40 minutes **makes** 3 cups
nutritional count per tablespoon 3.3g total fat
(0.6g saturated fat); 165kJ (39 cal); 2g carbohydrate;
0.5g protein; 0.3g fibre

note We used Russet Burbank potatoes, also known as Idaho.
You can use other floury varieties such as sebago or coliban.

serving suggestions Pitta bread and raw vegetable sticks.

lamb fillo rolls

⅓ cup (80ml) olive oil
1 small brown onion (80g), chopped finely
250g (8 ounces) minced (ground) lamb
2 tablespoons dried currants
1 teaspoon ground cinnamon
½ teaspoon freshly grated nutmeg
⅓ cup (80ml) dry red wine
1 tablespoon tomato paste
2 tablespoons roasted pine nuts
2 tablespoons finely chopped fresh
  flat-leaf parsley
10 sheets fillo pastry

1 Heat 1 tablespoon of the oil in large frying pan; cook onion, stirring, until softened. Add lamb; cook, stirring, until browned. Stir in currants and spices. Add combined wine and paste; bring to the boil. Reduce heat; simmer, uncovered, until liquid evaporates. Cool. Stir in nuts and parsley.
2 Preheat oven to 220°C/425°F. Oil oven trays, line with baking paper.
3 Brush 1 sheet of pastry with some of the remaining oil; top with a second sheet. Cut layered sheets into four strips. Press a level tablespoon of lamb mixture in a log shape along base of one narrow edge of pastry strip, leaving 1cm (½-inch) border. Roll pastry over filling; fold in sides then roll up to make a log shape. Repeat to make 20 rolls.
4 Place rolls, seam-side down, about 2cm (¾ inch) apart, on trays. Brush rolls with a little more oil.
5 Bake fillo rolls about 15 minutes or until browned lightly.

prep + cook time 40 minutes (+ cooling) **makes** 20
nutritional count per roll 6.6g total fat (1.3g saturated fat); 407kJ (97 cal); 5.5g carbohydrate; 3.7g protein; 0.5g fibre

note When working with the first two sheets of pastry, cover the remaining pastry with a sheet of baking paper then a damp tea towel to prevent it from drying out.

prawn and haloumi kebabs

90g (3 ounces) haloumi cheese
18 small uncooked prawns (shrimp) (450g),
  shelled, deveined
2 teaspoons rigani
2 tablespoons olive oil
6 bay leaves, halved

1 Cut cheese into 12 bite-sized pieces. Combine
cheese, prawns, rigani and oil in shallow bowl.
Thread prawns, bay leaves and cheese alternately
onto 6 small skewers; season with pepper.
2 Cook skewers on heated grill plate (or grill or
barbecue or grill pan) over medium-high heat until
prawns are cooked through.

prep + cook time 20 minutes **makes** 6
nutritional count per skewer 8.9g total fat (2.7g
saturated fat); 520kJ (124 cal); 0.3g carbohydrate;
10.9g protein; 0.1g fibre

note Soak bamboo skewers in cold water for 1 hour
before using to prevent them scorching during cooking.

serving suggestions Lemon wedges and bread.

grilled eggplant with marjoram vinaigrette

1 large eggplant (500g), sliced into
  5mm (¼-inch) rounds
¾ cup (180ml) olive oil
1 small red onion (100g), sliced thinly
¼ cup (60ml) sherry vinegar
2 teaspoons caster (superfine) sugar
2 tablespoons finely chopped fresh marjoram

1 Preheat oven to 200°C/400°F. Line baking trays with baking paper.
2 Brush both sides of eggplant slices with ¼ cup of the oil; place slices, in single layer, on trays.
3 Bake eggplant about 25 minutes, turning halfway through, until browned.
4 Meanwhile, combine remaining oil with remaining ingredients in small bowl.
5 Spoon vinaigrette over eggplant. Serve eggplant warm or at room temperature.

prep + cook time 50 minutes **serves** 6
nutritional count per serving 28.3g total fat (4g saturated fat); 1112kJ (278 cal); 4.6g carbohydrate; 1.2g protein; 2.2g fibre

note Marjoram has a sweet pine and citrus flavour. You can use fresh oregano instead.

serving suggestion Crusty bread.

marinated mushrooms

2 cups (500ml) white wine vinegar
½ cup (125ml) dry white wine
1 cup (250ml) water
4 bay leaves
2 tablespoons coarse cooking salt
750g (1½ pounds) baby button mushrooms
4 cloves garlic, sliced thickly
1 teaspoon black peppercorns
3 sprigs rigani
1¼ cups (310ml) extra virgin olive oil

1 Sterilise 1 litre (4-cup) jar and lid (see notes).
2 Meanwhile, combine vinegar, wine, the water, bay leaves and salt in large saucepan; heat to simmer without boiling. Add mushrooms; simmer, uncovered, 10 minutes. Drain mushrooms, reserve bay leaves; discard liquid. Spread mushrooms in single layer on absorbent paper; stand 5 minutes.
3 Spoon mushrooms into hot sterilised jar with reserved bay leaves, garlic, peppercorns and rigani. Pour hot oil over mushrooms in jar, pressing on mushrooms with back of spoon to release any trapped air, leaving 1cm (½-inch) space between mushrooms and top of jar. Seal jar while hot.

prep + cook time 25 minutes (+ standing)
makes 4 cups
nutritional count per ¼ cup 1.9g total fat (0.3g saturated fat); 110kJ (26 cal); 0.7g carbohydrate; 1.6g protein; 0.7g fibre

notes To sterilise jars: wash the jar and lid in warm soapy water; rinse well. Place jar in large saucepan and cover with water. Bring to the boil and boil for 10 minutes. Carefully drain water from jars; transfer jar and lid to a baking tray lined with a clean tea towel. Cover with a sheet of foil and place in a low oven until dry. Use straight from oven. Store marinated mushrooms in refrigerator for up to three months. Sometimes garlic will discolour during storage. The garlic is still edible – and harmless – if this happens.

eggplant fritters with garlic yogurt

1 large eggplant (500g), cut into thick lengths
1 tablespoon coarse cooking salt
vegetable oil, for deep-frying
1 teaspoon rigani

OREGANO AND LEMON BATTER
½ cup (75g) plain (all-purpose) flour
⅔ cup (160ml) beer
1 tablespoon rigani
1 teaspoon finely grated lemon rind

GARLIC YOGURT
1 cup (280g) greek-style yogurt
1 clove garlic, crushed
1 tablespoon finely chopped fresh dill

1 Place eggplant in strainer over bowl, sprinkle with salt; stand 1 hour.
2 Meanwhile, make oregano and lemon batter.
3 Make garlic yogurt.
4 Heat oil in large saucepan or wok. Rinse eggplant under cold water, pat dry with absorbent paper. Dip eggplant into batter, shake away excess. Deep-fry eggplant, in batches, turning occasionally, about 5 minutes or until browned. Drain on absorbent paper.
5 Sprinkle eggplant with rigani and a little salt; serve with garlic yogurt.

OREGANO AND LEMON BATTER Sift flour into large bowl, gradually whisk in beer until batter is smooth. Add rigani and rind; season. Stand 1 hour.

GARLIC YOGURT Combine ingredients in small bowl; season to taste.

prep + cook time 40 minutes (+ standing) serves 4
nutritional count per serving 18g total fat (4.4g saturated fat); 1295kJ (309 cal); 27g carbohydrate; 6.9g protein; 4g fibre

grilled fetta and baby truss tomatoes

200g (6½ ounces) fetta cheese
275g (9 ounces) baby truss tomatoes
1 tablespoon olive oil
1 teaspoon rigani

1   Preheat griller (broiler).
2   Place cheese and tomatoes on oven tray. Drizzle with oil; sprinkle with rigani. Season with pepper.
3   Place cheese and tomatoes under grill about 8 minutes or until cheese is browned lightly.

prep + cook time 10 minutes **serves** 4
nutritional count per serving 16g total fat (8.2g saturated fat); 796kJ (190 cal); 1.8g carbohydrate; 9.4g protein; 0.9g fibre

serving suggestion Thinly sliced toasted bread stick.

note We used ling in this recipe, but any firm white fish fillets will be fine.

fish croquettes

1 medium brown onion (150g), quartered
8 cloves
2 cloves garlic, halved
2 bay leaves
2 cups (500ml) milk
500g (1 pound) skinless white fish fillets,
  chopped coarsely
3 medium potatoes (600g), chopped coarsely
½ cup (60g) seeded green olives,
  chopped coarsely
¾ cup (110g) plain (all-purpose) flour
15 canned, drained anchovy fillets,
  halved lengthways
vegetable oil, for deep-frying

1 Stud onion quarters with cloves. Place onion, garlic, bay leaves and milk in medium saucepan; bring to simmer, add fish, cook over low heat about 5 minutes. Remove fish from milk mixture to large bowl. Flake fish, discard bones.
2 Meanwhile, bring milk mixture to the boil, add potato; cook, covered, about 15 minutes or until tender. Remove potato from milk mixture, add to fish; mash coarsely. Strain milk mixture into jug; discard bay leaf and cloves from onion. Finely chop onion and garlic, add to fish mixture with olives. Stir sifted flour and ¾ cup (180ml) of the reserved milk into fish mixture, in several batches. Season.
3 Roll 2 heaped tablespoonfuls of fish mixture into balls; place on baking-paper-lined tray. Refrigerate 1 hour. Make an indent in balls, push a rolled-up anchovy half inside each ball; roll balls into ovals to enclose anchovies.
4 Heat oil in large saucepan or wok. Deep-fry croquettes, in batches, until browned; drain on absorbent paper.
5 Serve croquettes with lemon wedges.

prep + cook time 1 hour 20 minutes (+ refrigeration)
makes 30
nutritional count per croquette 5.2g total fat (1g saturated fat); 385kJ (92 cal); 5.8g carbohydrate; 5.3g protein; 0.6g fibre

deep-fried baby calamari

500g (1 pound) baby calamari, cleaned
⅓ cup (50g) plain (all-purpose) flour
vegetable oil, for deep-frying
2 teaspoons rigani

1 Slice calamari into thin rings. Season flour with salt and pepper.
2 Heat oil in medium saucepan or wok. Toss calamari in flour mixture; shake away excess. Deep-fry calamari, in batches, until browned lightly and tender. Drain on absorbent paper. Sprinkle with rigani; serve with a squeeze of lemon juice.

prep + cook time 15 minutes **serves** 4
nutritional count per serving 4g total fat (0.6g saturated fat); 425kJ (100 cal); 6.4g carbohydrate; 9.9g protein; 0.4g fibre

notes Don't overcook the calamari or it will toughen. It should take about 30 seconds to cook one small batch at a time. Reheat the oil before frying the next batch of calamari.
Ask the fishmonger to clean the calamari for you.

serving suggestion Lemon wedges.

pan-fried haloumi

200g (6½ ounces) haloumi cheese
2 tablespoons olive oil
2 teaspoons rigani

1 Cut cheese into slices.
2 Combine haloumi, oil and rigani in shallow bowl; season with pepper. Stand 30 minutes.
3 Drain oil mixture from haloumi into large frying pan; heat oil, cook cheese until browned lightly. Serve immediately.

prep + cook time 5 minutes (+ standing) **serves** 4
nutritional count per serving 17.7g total fat (7g saturated fat); 853kJ (204 cal); 0.9g carbohydrate; 10.7g protein; 0.1g fibre

note Fried haloumi needs to be eaten as soon as possible after cooking as it becomes chewy as it cools. It only takes a minute or so to fry, so this dish must be prepared just before serving.

chickpea patties with tahini sauce

400g (12½ ounces) canned chickpeas
  (garbanzo beans), rinsed, drained
½ small brown onion (40g), chopped coarsely
1 egg
½ cup (50g) coarsely grated kasseri cheese
¼ cup coarsely chopped fresh oregano
1 clove garlic, crushed
1 tablespoon olive oil
½ cup (35g) stale breadcrumbs
2 tablespoons olive oil, extra

TAHINI SAUCE
2 tablespoons finely chopped fresh
  flat-leaf parsley
2 tablespoons tahini
2 tablespoons hot water
1 tablespoon olive oil
1 tablespoon lemon juice
1 clove garlic, crushed

1 Process chickpeas, onion, egg, cheese, oregano, garlic and olive oil until thick. Transfer mixture to medium bowl; stir in breadcrumbs. Season to taste; stand 10 minutes.
2 Meanwhile, make tahini sauce.
3 With wet hands, shape level tablespoons of mixture into patties.
4 Heat extra oil in large frying pan; cook patties about 2 minutes each side or until browned. Drain on absorbent paper.
5 Serve patties with sauce.

TAHINI SAUCE Combine ingredients in small bowl; season to taste.

prep + cook time 30 minutes (+ standing)
makes 22
nutritional count per patty 4.6g total fat (0.9g saturated fat); 232kJ (55 cal); 1.9g carbohydrate; 1.8g protein; 0.7g fibre

note Raw artichokes can stain your hands, so wear plastic gloves when preparing them.

braised artichokes with crunchy almond topping

6 large globe artichokes (2.4kg)
4 bay leaves
4 cloves garlic
1 litre (4 cups) chicken stock

CRUNCHY ALMOND TOPPING
¾ cup (50g) fresh breadcrumbs
⅓ cup (25g) flaked almonds
½ cup (60g) seeded green olives,
  chopped finely
¼ cup (60ml) olive oil
2 tablespoons finely chopped fresh
  flat-leaf parsley
1 tablespoon finely grated lemon rind
2 tablespoons lemon juice

1 Preheat oven to 200°C/400°F.
2 Prepare artichokes by snapping off tough outer leaves and peeling stems. Trim stems to 5cm (2 inches). Cut 2cm (¾ inch) off top of artichokes to reveal chokes. Cut artichokes in half from top to bottom, then scoop out and discard furry chokes from the centres. As you finish preparing each artichoke, place it in a large bowl of water containing the juice of about half a lemon (this stops any discolouration while you are preparing the next one).
3 Drain artichokes. Combine artichokes, leaves, garlic and stock in small baking dish, ensuring artichokes are covered with stock. Bake, covered, about 45 minutes or until artichokes are tender.
4 Meanwhile, make crunchy almond topping.
5 Drain artichokes; discard liquid. Serve artichokes hot or at room temperature sprinkled with topping.

CRUNCHY ALMOND TOPPING Combine breadcrumbs and nuts on oven tray; roast about 5 minutes or until golden. Cool 5 minutes. Combine breadcrumb mixture with remaining ingredients in small bowl.

prep + cook time 1 hour 40 minutes **serves** 6
nutritional count per serving 13.1g total fat (1.9g saturated fat); 928kJ (222 cal); 13.1g carbohydrate; 11.6g protein; 3.3g fibre

thyme and garlic marinated olives

1 medium lemon (140g)
½ cup (125ml) olive oil
2 cloves garlic, bruised
3 sprigs fresh thyme
1 bay leaf
2 cups (320g) large kalamata olives,
  rinsed, drained

1 Sterilise jar and lid (see notes).
2 Meanwhile, using a vegetable peeler, peel rind thinly from lemon, avoiding white pith. Combine rind, oil, garlic, thyme and bay leaf in medium saucepan over medium heat; heat until warm and garlic begins to sizzle. Add olives; cook over low heat 10 minutes.
3 Spoon hot olives into sterilised jar. Seal jar while hot.

prep + cook time 15 minutes (+ standing)
serves 12
nutritional count per serving 7.4g total fat (1g saturated fat); 295kJ (70 cal); 0.6g carbohydrate; 0.4g protein; 0.7g fibre

notes To sterilise jars: wash the jar and lid in warm soapy water; rinse well. Place jar in large saucepan and cover with water. Bring to the boil and boil for 10 minutes. Carefully drain water from jars; transfer jar and lid to a baking tray lined with a clean tea towel. Cover with a sheet of foil and place in a low oven until dry. Use straight from oven.
Serve olives warm if you like or store olives in refrigerator for one week.
Look for large "meaty" olives from delicatessens as they have a firm texture.

octopus salad with grilled tomatoes

4 large egg tomatoes (360g), halved
1 tablespoon fresh thyme leaves
2 tablespoons olive oil
1kg (2 pounds) cleaned baby octopus
270g (8½ ounces) bottled char-grilled red
  capsicum (bell pepper), drained, sliced thinly
1 medium oak leaf lettuce, torn
2 tablespoons rinsed, drained capers,
  chopped coarsely
2 lebanese cucumbers (260g), chopped coarsely
½ cup (75g) seeded black olives,
  chopped coarsely
½ cup coarsely chopped fresh flat-leaf parsley
¼ cup (60ml) lemon juice
1 clove garlic, crushed

1 Place tomato, thyme and half the oil in medium
bowl; toss gently to combine. Cook on heated
oiled flat plate, uncovered, until just softened and
browned lightly.
2 Meanwhile, cook octopus on heated oiled grill
plate (or grill or barbecue), brushing with remaining
oil, until tender.
3 Place octopus in large bowl with remaining
ingredients; toss gently to combine. Serve salad
with grilled tomato.

prep + cook time 20 minutes **serves** 4
nutritional count per serving 14.4g total fat (1.6g
saturated fat); 1455kJ (348 cal); 9.7g carbohydrate;
43g protein; 3.1g fibre

spanakopita

1.5kg (3 pounds) silver beet (swiss chard),
 trimmed
1 tablespoon olive oil
1 medium brown onion (150g), chopped finely
2 cloves garlic, crushed
1 teaspoon ground nutmeg
200g (6½ ounces) fetta cheese, crumbled
1 tablespoon finely grated lemon rind
¼ cup each coarsely chopped fresh mint,
 fresh flat-leaf parsley and fresh dill
4 green onions (scallions), chopped finely
16 sheets fillo pastry
125g (4 ounces) butter, melted
2 teaspoons sesame seeds

1 Boil, steam or microwave silver beet until just wilted; drain. Squeeze out excess moisture; drain on absorbent paper. Chop silver beet coarsely; spread out on absorbent paper.
2 Heat oil in small frying pan; cook brown onion and garlic, stirring, until onion is soft. Add nutmeg; cook, stirring, until fragrant. Combine onion mixture and silver beet in large bowl with fetta, rind, herbs and green onion.
3 Preheat oven to 180°C/350°F. Oil oven trays.
4 Brush 1 sheet of pastry with some of the butter; fold lengthways into thirds, brushing with butter between each fold. Place rounded tablespoon of silver beet mixture at the bottom of one narrow edge of folded pastry sheet, leaving a border. Fold one corner of pastry diagonally over filling to form a large triangle. Continue folding to end of pastry sheet, retaining triangular shape. Repeat with remaining ingredients to make 16 triangles in total.
5 Place triangles, seam-side down, on trays. Brush with remaining butter; sprinkle with sesame seeds. Bake about 15 minutes or until browned lightly.

prep + cook time 50 minutes makes 16
nutritional count per triangle 11.1g total fat (6.4g saturated fat); 690kJ (165 cal); 11g carbohydrate; 4.7g protein; 1.5g fibre

notes Spanakopita comes from the Greek words spanaki (spinach) and pitta (pie).
When working with the first sheet of pastry, cover remaining pastry with a sheet of baking paper then a damp tea towel to prevent it from drying out.

beetroot salad

500g (1 pound) bunch baby beetroot (beets)
2 tablespoons olive oil
1 tablespoon red wine vinegar
1 tablespoon finely chopped fresh flat-leaf parsley
1 teaspoon finely chopped fresh dill
1 clove garlic, crushed

1 Discard leaves from beetroot; reserve stems. Wash beetroot and stems. Place beetroots in medium saucepan; cover with water. Bring to the boil; simmer, covered, about 30 minutes or until tender. Add stems 5 minutes before end of cooking time. Drain.
2 When beetroots are cool enough to handle, use disposable gloves to gently slip off skin from beetroots; discard skins. Slice beetroots and stems. Combine beetroots and stems in shallow bowl with combined remaining ingredients; season to taste.

prep + cook time 40 minutes (+ cooling) **serves** 4
nutritional count per serving 4.6g total fat (0.7g saturated fat); 260kJ (62 cal); 4.3g carbohydrate; 1g protein; 2g fibre

note Use disposable gloves when handling beetroot to prevent your hands becoming stained.

cheese fillo triangles

1 cup (200g) cottage cheese
100g (3 ounces) fetta cheese
1 egg
2 tablespoons each finely chopped fresh
  oregano and flat-leaf parsley
15 sheets fillo pastry
¼ cup (60ml) olive oil

1 Preheat oven to 220°C/425°F. Oil oven trays,
line with baking paper.
2 Combine cheeses, egg and herbs in medium
bowl; season with pepper.
3 Brush 1 sheet of pasty with some of the oil;
top with 2 more sheets, brushing each with more
oil. Cut layered sheets into 3 strips lengthways.
Place 1 level tablespoon of cheese mixture at one
narrow edge of each pastry strip. Fold one corner
of pastry diagonally over filling to form a triangle.
Continue folding to end of strip, retaining
triangular shape. Repeat to make 15 triangles.
4 Place triangles, seam-side down, on trays;
brush with a little more oil. Bake triangles about
15 minutes or until browned lightly.

prep + cook time 30 minutes **makes** 15
nutritional count per triangle 6.5g total fat (2.2g
saturated fat); 480kJ (115 cal); 9g carbohydrate;
5g protein; 0.4g fibre

note When working with the first three sheets of pastry,
cover remaining pastry with a sheet of baking paper
then a damp tea towel to prevent it from drying out.

harvest of the sea

prawn souvlakia with tomato and fennel sauce

16 large uncooked prawns (shrimp) (1.1kg)
2 tablespoons olive oil
3 cloves garlic, crushed
2 teaspoons dried mint
1 teaspoon finely grated lemon rind
2 tablespoons lemon juice

TOMATO AND FENNEL SAUCE
2 baby fennel bulbs (260g)
1 tablespoon olive oil
1 medium brown onion (150g), chopped finely
2 cloves garlic, chopped finely
3 medium ripe tomatoes (450g), chopped coarsely
¼ cup (60ml) ouzo or pernod
1 cup coarsely chopped fresh mint

1 Shell and devein prawns, leaving tails intact. Combine prawns in large bowl with remaining ingredients. Cover; refrigerate 1 hour.
2 Make tomato and fennel sauce.
3 Thread prawns onto eight metal skewers; reserve marinade. Cook prawn skewers on heated oiled grill plate (or grill or barbecue or grill pan), brushing with reserved marinade, until cooked through.
4 Serve prawns with sauce.

TOMATO AND FENNEL SAUCE Reserve fennel fronds; chop fennel and fronds finely, separately. Heat oil in medium saucepan over medium heat; cook onion, garlic and fennel until softened. Add tomato and ouzo; cook until heated through. Just before serving, stir in fronds and mint; season.

prep + cook time 35 minutes (+ refrigeration)
makes 8
nutritional count per skewer 7.5g total fat (1.3g saturated fat); 702kJ (168 cal); 5.9g carbohydrate; 15.4g protein; 2g fibre

serving suggestion Rice pilaf.

barbecued vine-leaf-wrapped sardines

12 small whole sardines (500g), cleaned
1 medium lemon (140g), halved, sliced thinly
12 fresh bay leaves
12 small preserved grape leaves
1 tablespoon olive oil

GARLIC AND LEMON POTATOES
2 tablespoons olive oil
600g (1¼ pounds) small potatoes, sliced thinly
1 medium lemon (140g)
4 cloves garlic, sliced thinly

1 Rinse cavities of sardines, pat dry. Season cavities; top each sardine with a lemon slice and a bay leaf. Wrap each sardine tightly in a grape leaf to enclose lemon and bay leaf, leaving heads and tails exposed. Brush sardines with oil.
2 Make garlic and lemon potatoes.
3 Meanwhile, cook sardines on heated oiled grill plate (or grill or barbecue or grill pan), until cooked through.
4 Serve sardines with potatoes and lemon wedges.

GARLIC AND LEMON POTATOES Heat oil in large frying pan; cook potatoes, turning, about 15 minutes until starting to soften and brown. Remove rind from whole lemon using a zester, add to potatoes with garlic; cook, stirring, until potatoes and garlic are cooked through. Season to taste.

prep + cook time 1 hour serves 4
nutritional count per serving 20g total fat (3.9g saturated fat); 1686kJ (403 cal); 17g carbohydrate; 37.9g protein; 3.6g fibre

note Preserved grape leaves are available in cryovac packets from some delicatessens and Middle Eastern food shops; they must be rinsed well and dried before using.

serving suggestion Sliced tomato and white onion salad.

fish steaks with kalamata olive dressing

4 x 200g (6½-ounce) white fish steaks
2 teaspoons olive oil
1 cup coarsely chopped fresh flat-leaf parsley

KALAMATA OLIVE DRESSING
1 medium red onion (170g), sliced thinly
1 cup (150g) seeded kalamata olives,
  chopped coarsely
8 anchovies (20g), drained,
  sliced thinly lengthways
1 tablespoon rigani
1 clove garlic, crushed
¼ cup (60ml) red wine vinegar
¼ cup (60ml) olive oil

1   Make kalamata olive dressing.
2   Brush steaks with oil; season. Cook steaks on heated grill plate (or grill or barbecue or grill pan) until cooked through.
3   Meanwhile, warm dressing in small saucepan; stir in parsley.
4   Serve steaks with dressing.

KALAMATA OLIVE DRESSING Combine ingredients in medium bowl; season.

prep + cook time 20 minutes **serves** 4
nutritional count per serving 26g total fat (4.1g saturated fat); 1250kJ (299 cal); 2.9g carbohydrate; 13.1g protein; 2.9g fibre

notes We used swordfish in this recipe; tuna steaks and firm white fish cutlets would also be fine. The dressing can be made a day ahead, cover, store in the refrigerator.

serving suggestion Garlic and lemon potatoes (see recipe page 42).

tuna souvlakia with char-grilled capsicum salad

600g (1¼-pound) piece tuna
1½ tablespoons olive oil
1 tablespoon rigani
1 teaspoon dried chilli flakes

CHAR-GRILLED CAPSICUM SALAD
3 medium red capsicums (bell peppers) (600g)
3 medium yellow capsicums (bell peppers) (600g)
3 cloves garlic, sliced thinly
¾ cup loosely packed fresh oregano leaves
2 tablespoons red wine vinegar

1 Cut tuna into 3cm (1¼-inch) pieces. Combine tuna, oil, rigani and chilli in medium bowl; season. Thread tuna onto eight metal skewers; place in shallow dish, cover, refrigerate 30 minutes.
2 Meanwhile, make char-grilled capsicum salad.
3 Cook tuna on heated grill plate (or grill or barbecue or grill pan), until cooked as desired.
4 Serve tuna with salad.

CHAR-GRILLED CAPSICUM SALAD Cook capsicums on heated grill plate (or grill or barbecue or grill pan) over high heat, turning, until skin blackens. Place capsicums in large bowl, cover with plastic; cool. Peel away skin, then slice capsicum thinly. Place capsicum in medium bowl with garlic, oregano and vinegar; toss gently to combine. Season to taste.

prep + cook time 40 minutes (+ cooling) serves 4
nutritional count per serving 9g total fat (1.4g saturated fat); 1155kJ (275 cal); 8.9g carbohydrate; 39.1g protein; 5.4g fibre

oven-roasted fish with braised fennel

2 baby fennel bulbs (260g)
2 tablespoons olive oil
1 medium red onion (170g), cut into thin wedges
1 cup (100g) large seeded green olives
1 medium lemon (140g)
1 cup (250ml) dry white wine
½ cup (125ml) fish stock
4 x 200g (6½-ounce) skinless white fish fillets

1   Preheat oven to 180°C/350°F.
2   Remove fennel fronds from tops of bulbs;
chop coarsely, reserve. Slice fennel bulbs thickly
lengthways.
3   Heat half the oil in medium baking dish over
heat. Cook fennel, onion and olives, stirring, until
browned lightly. Remove rind from lemon with
zester, add to dish with wine and stock; bring to
the boil. Transfer dish to oven; cook, uncovered,
about 10 minutes or until fennel is soft. Season.
4   Meanwhile, heat remaining oil in medium frying
pan. Pat fish dry; season. Brown fish lightly both
sides – do not cook through.
5   Increase oven to 200°C/400°F. Place fish on top
of fennel mixture; cook in oven about 5 minutes or
until fish is cooked through. Serve sprinkled with
reserved fennel fronds.

prep + cook time 35 minutes **serves** 4
nutritional count per serving 20.8g total fat (4g
saturated fat); 1620kJ (387 cal); 4.5g carbohydrate;
42g protein; 2.3g fibre

note We used blue eye in this recipe, but any
white fish fillet will be fine.

prawn, zucchini and mint pilaf

20 uncooked medium prawns (shrimp) (1kg)
60g (2 ounces) butter
1 tablespoon olive oil
1 medium white onion (150g), chopped finely
2 cloves garlic, chopped finely
1 fresh small red chilli, chopped finely
1½ cups (300g) white long-grain rice
1 teaspoon finely grated lemon rind
¼ cup (60ml) dry white wine
1½ cups (375ml) hot fish stock
3 medium zucchini (360g), grated coarsely

MINTED LEMON DRESSING
2 medium lemons (280g), peeled, segmented
1 cup loosely packed fresh flat-leaf parsley leaves
½ cup loosely packed fresh mint leaves
¼ cup (60ml) olive oil

1 Shell and devein prawns, leaving tails intact; refrigerate.
2 Heat butter and oil in medium heavy-based saucepan; cook onion, garlic and chilli, stirring, until onion softens. Add rice, rind and wine; cook until liquid has evaporated. Stir in hot stock, bring to the boil. Reduce heat to low, stirring; cook, covered, 10 minutes.
3 Meanwhile, make minted lemon dressing.
4 Stir zucchini into rice mixture; top with prawns. Cover; cook 5 minutes. Remove from heat; stand, covered, 5 minutes.
5 Serve pilaf drizzled with dressing.

MINTED LEMON DRESSING Process ingredients until chopped finely. Season to taste.

prep + cook time 40 minutes (+ standing) serves 4
nutritional count per serving 32.3g total fat (11.2g saturated fat); 2880kJ (688 cal); 64.2g carbohydrate; 33.2g protein; 4.6g fibre

oven-baked fish with tomato and olives

4 x 260g (8½-ounce) whole white fish
1 tablespoon olive oil
2 medium red onions (340g), sliced thinly
2 stalks celery (300g), trimmed, sliced thinly
4 cloves garlic, sliced thinly
400g (12½ ounces) cherry tomatoes
¾ cup (120g) seeded black olives
1 medium lemon (140g), halved, sliced thinly
¼ cup fresh rosemary sprigs
1 cup (250ml) dry white wine
½ cup coarsely chopped fresh flat-leaf parsley

1 Preheat oven to 200°C/400°F.
2 Remove heads from fish; clean fish.
3 Heat oil in medium baking dish; cook onion, celery and garlic, stirring, until browned lightly. Add tomatoes, olives, lemon and rosemary.
4 Season fish; place on vegetables. Pour wine over fish. Roast, uncovered, about 15 minutes or until fish is cooked through.
5 Serve fish sprinkled with parsley.

prep + cook time 40 minutes **serves** 4
nutritional count per serving 2.9g total fat (0.5g saturated fat); 253kJ (60 cal); 1.8g carbohydrate; 5.9g protein; 1.3g fibre

note We used plate-sized leather jackets in this recipe, but any white fish will be fine.

serving suggestions Potato, pasta or rice salad.

squid stuffed with rice, currants and pine nuts

12 small squid (800g)
¼ cup (60ml) olive oil
1 medium onion (150g), chopped finely
2 cloves garlic, chopped finely
½ cup (100g) white long-grain rice
¾ cup (180ml) fish stock
2 tablespoons dried currants
2 tablespoons roasted pine nuts
25g (¾ ounce) baby spinach leaves, sliced thinly
1 tablespoon finely shredded fresh mint leaves
1 teaspoon finely grated lemon rind
2 tablespoons lemon juice

1 Clean squid; reserve tentacles and wing. Cut tentacles and wings into small pieces.
2 Heat 1 tablespoon of the oil in medium heavy-based saucepan; cook onion and garlic, stirring, until onion softens. Add rice; stir to coat in onion mixture. Stir in squid pieces, stock, currants and pine nuts. Simmer, covered tightly, about 10 minutes or until liquid has evaporated and rice is tender.
3 Stir spinach, mint, rind and juice into rice mixture; season. Spoon rounded tablespoons mixture into squid tubes leaving 1cm (½-inch) gap; secure ends with toothpicks.
4 Preheat oven to 180°C/350°F.
5 Heat remaining oil in large frying pan; cook squid, in batches, until browned lightly. Transfer squid to oven tray, roast uncovered, about 5 minutes or until squid is opaque and filling is heated through.

prep + cook time 1 hour serves 4
nutritional count per serving 20.2g total fat (2.9g saturated fat); 1505kJ (360 cal); 26.6g carbohydrate; 18.3g protein; 2.1g fibre

serving suggestion Baby rocket salad.

tomato and oregano prawns

1kg (2 pounds) uncooked medium
  tiger prawns (shrimp)
2 tablespoons olive oil
8 green onions (scallions), sliced thinly
4 cloves garlic, sliced thinly
½ cup (125ml) dry white wine
700g (1½-pound) bottled tomato pasta sauce
2 tablespoons coarsely chopped fresh
  oregano leaves

1   Shell and devein prawns, leaving tails intact.
2   Heat oil in large frying pan; cook prawns,
onion and garlic, in two batches, until prawns
are changed in colour. Remove from pan; transfer
to large bowl.
3   Add wine to same heated pan; simmer until
liquid is reduced by half. Add pasta sauce;
bring to the boil. Reduce heat; simmer, uncovered,
about 5 minutes or until sauce is thickened.
4   Return prawn mixture to sauce with oregano;
stir gently until prawns are heated through.

prep + cook time 30 minutes **serves** 4
nutritional count per serving 3.1g total fat (0.4g
saturated fat); 364kJ (87 cal); 5g carbohydrate;
7.8g protein; 1.1g fibre

serving suggestions Orzo or risoni pasta.

notes We used blue-eye for this recipe. Soak bamboo skewers in water for 1 hour before using to prevent them scorching during cooking.

herbed fish skewers
with potato smash and skordalia

800g (1½ pounds) white fish fillets,
  cut into 2cm (¾-inch) pieces
¼ cup (60ml) olive oil
2 tablespoons each finely chopped fresh
  flat-leaf parsley and lemon thyme
1kg (2 pounds) baby new potatoes, unpeeled
½ cup (120g) sour cream
40g (1½ ounces) butter, softened

SKORDALIA
1 small potato (120g)
1 slice white bread
2 cloves garlic, crushed
1 tablespoon cider vinegar
¼ cup (60ml) water
2 tablespoons olive oil

1 Thread fish onto eight skewers; place in medium shallow dish. Brush with combined oil and herbs. Cover; refrigerate 20 minutes.
2 Meanwhile, make skordalia.
3 Boil, steam or microwave potatoes until tender; drain. Mash half the potatoes in medium bowl with sour cream and butter until smooth. Using fork, crush remaining potatoes until skins burst; fold into mash mixture. Cover to keep warm.
4 Cook skewers on heated oiled grill plate (or grill or barbecue). Serve skewers with smash and skordalia.

SKORDALIA Boil, steam or microwave potato until tender; drain. Mash potato in medium bowl until smooth. Discard crusts from bread. Soak bread in small bowl of cold water; drain. Squeeze out excess liquid. Blend or process bread with remaining ingredients until smooth; stir mixture into potato.

prep + cook time 50 minutes (+ refrigeration)
serves 4
nutritional count per serving 44.7g total fat (16.7g saturated fat); 3114kJ (745 cal); 39.8g carbohydrate; 42.9g protein; 5.3g fibre

salt cod and potato pie

1.5kg (3 pounds) salt cod
2 tablespoons olive oil
2 medium brown onions (300g), sliced thinly
4 cloves garlic, crushed
1½ cups (300g) white long-grain rice
1 cup coarsely chopped fresh flat-leaf parsley
½ cup coarsely chopped fresh dill
8 small potatoes (800g), sliced thinly
1.5 litres (6 cups) fish stock
2 tablespoons coarsely chopped flat-leaf parsley, extra

1 Soak cod in cold water for 8 hours, changing the water twice.
2 Heat oil in large frying pan; cook onion and garlic, stirring, until onion softens. Transfer to bowl; stir in rice and herbs. Season with pepper.
3 Preheat oven to 200°C/400°F. Drain cod. Remove skin, cut cod into large pieces, discarding any bones; gently stir into rice mixture.
4 Cover base of deep 4-litre (16-cup) ovenproof dish with one-third of the potato. Top with half the fish mixture; repeat layers with remaining potato and fish mixture, ending with potato. Place dish on oven tray, pour stock into dish.
5 Bake pie, uncovered, about 1¾ hours or until potatoes are tender. Stand 10 minutes. Sprinkle with extra parsley before serving.

prep + cook time 2 hours 30 minutes (+ standing)
serves 8
nutritional count per serving 9.9g total fat (1.5g saturated fat); 3215kJ (768 cal); 44g carbohydrate; 118g protein; 3.5g fibre

notes You will need to start this recipe 24 hours ahead. Salt cod is available from most Greek, Italian and Portuguese delicatessens and fishmongers.

octopus in red wine

1.5kg (3 pounds) octopus tentacles
1½ cups (375ml) dry red wine
¼ cup (60ml) red wine vinegar
¼ cup (60ml) olive oil
2 cloves garlic, sliced thinly
2 bay leaves
1 fresh small red chilli, sliced
1 cinnamon stick
2 teaspoons whole allspice
2 strips lemon rind
1½ cups (375ml) water
12 baby brown pickling onions (240g)
8 baby chat potatoes (240g)
1 cup coarsely chopped fresh flat-leaf parsley

1 Preheat oven to 120°C/250°F.
2 Combine octopus, wine, vinegar, oil, garlic, bay leaves, chilli, cinnamon, allspice, rind and the water in large deep flameproof dish. Cook, covered, in oven 1 hour. Add onions to dish, cook, covered, about 30 minutes or until tender.
3 Remove octopus and onions from dish. Bring liquid in dish to the boil; add potatoes, simmer, uncovered, about 20 minutes or until potatoes are tender. Remove potatoes, cut in half. Simmer sauce, uncovered, about 15 minutes or until sauce is reduced to about 2 cups.
4 Meanwhile, thickly slice octopus. Add to sauce with onions and potatoes, cook until heated through. Just before serving, add parsley. Season to taste.

prep + cook time 2 hours 20 minutes serves 6
nutritional count per serving 11.7g total fat (2g saturated fat); 1421kJ (339 cal); 12.5g carbohydrate; 65.6g protein; 2.3g fibre

serving suggestion Crusty bread.

note We used barramundi in this recipe, but any white fish fillets would be fine.

crisp-skinned fish with roast garlic skordalia

4 x 200g (6½-ounce) white fish fillets,
 skin on

ROSEMARY OIL
¼ cup (60ml) olive oil
4 cloves garlic, sliced thinly
2 tablespoons rosemary

ROAST GARLIC SKORDALIA
2 medium bulbs garlic (140g)
600g (1¼ pounds) small potatoes
½ cup (125ml) milk, warmed
1 tablespoon finely grated lemon rind
½ cup (125ml) olive oil
½ cup (140g) greek-style yogurt
¼ cup (60ml) lemon juice

1 Make rosemary oil and roast garlic skordalia.
2 Pat fish dry with absorbent paper; season. Heat 1 tablespoon of the rosemary oil in medium frying pan; cook fish, skin-side down, about 2 minutes or until skin is crisp. Turn fish, cook fish through.
3 Serve fish with skordalia and drizzled with rosemary oil.

ROSEMARY OIL Heat oil, garlic and rosemary in small saucepan over low heat until garlic begins to colour. Cool.

ROAST GARLIC SKORDALIA Preheat oven to 220°C/425°F. Wrap garlic in foil; place on oven tray with potatoes. Roast about 30 minutes or until garlic and potatoes are soft. Stand until cool enough to handle. Peel potatoes; place flesh in medium bowl. Squeeze garlic from cloves, add to potatoes with half the warm milk. Mash rind, garlic and potatoes until smooth. Gradually stir in oil, 1 tablespoon at a time. Stir in yogurt and juice; season to taste. Just before serving, heat remaining milk in medium saucepan; add skordalia, cook, stirring, until heated through.

prep + cook time 1 hour (+ cooling) **serves** 4
nutritional count per serving 53.4g total fat (11g saturated fat); 3210kJ (767 cal); 24g carbohydrate; 47.7g protein; 6.7g fibre

village favourites

slow-roasted lamb with skordalia and potatoes

2kg (4-pound) leg of lamb
2 cloves garlic, crushed
½ cup (125ml) lemon juice
2 tablespoons olive oil
1 tablespoon fresh oregano leaves
2 teaspoons fresh lemon thyme leaves
5 large potatoes (1.5kg), chopped coarsely
1 tablespoon finely grated lemon rind
2 tablespoons each lemon juice, olive oil, extra

SKORDALIA
1 medium potato (200g), quartered
3 cloves garlic, crushed
1 tablespoon lemon juice
1 tablespoon white wine vinegar
2 tablespoons water
⅓ cup (80ml) olive oil

1 Combine lamb, garlic, juice, oil, oregano and half the thyme in large bowl. Cover; refrigerate 3 hours or overnight.
2 Preheat oven to 160°C/325°F.
3 Place lamb mixture in large baking dish; roast, uncovered, 3 hours.
4 Meanwhile, make skordalia.
5 Combine potatoes, rind, extra juice, extra oil and remaining thyme in large bowl. Place potatoes, in single layer, on oven tray. Roast potatoes, uncovered, for last 30 minutes of lamb cooking time.
6 Remove lamb from oven; cover to keep warm.
7 Increase oven to 220°C/425°F; roast potatoes a further 20 minutes or until browned lightly and cooked through.
8 Serve lamb and potatoes with skordalia and pan juices.

SKORDALIA Boil, steam or microwave potato until tender; drain. Push potato through fine sieve into medium bowl; cool 10 minutes. Whisk combined garlic, juice, vinegar and the water into potato. Gradually whisk in oil in a thin, steady stream; continue whisking until skordalia thickens. Stir in about a tablespoon of warm water if skordalia becomes too thick.

prep + cook time 4 hours (+ refrigeration) **serves** 4
nutritional count per serving 57g total fat (14g saturated fat); 4556kJ (1090 cal); 51.5g carbohydrate; 91.2g protein; 6.7g fibre

rabbit stifado

1.4kg (2¾-pound) whole rabbit
⅔ cup (160ml) dry red wine
⅓ cup (80ml) red wine vinegar
2 cloves garlic, crushed
3 bay leaves
1 cinnamon stick
6 cloves
1 tablespoon light brown sugar
2 teaspoons rigani
½ teaspoon ground allspice
¼ cup (60ml) olive oil
800g (1½ pounds) baby brown onions, peeled
2 tablespoons tomato paste
1 litre (4 cups) water
2 tablespoons coarsely chopped fresh
  flat-leaf parsley

1 Chop rabbit into eight even-sized pieces. Combine rabbit, wine, vinegar, garlic, bay leaves, cinnamon, cloves, sugar, rigani and allspice in large bowl. Cover; refrigerate 3 hours or overnight.
2 Heat oil in large saucepan; cook onions, stirring, over medium heat, until softened. Remove from pan.
3 Remove rabbit from marinade; reserve marinade. Cook rabbit in same heated pan, in batches, until browned. Remove from pan.
4 Return rabbit and onions to pan with paste, the water and reserved marinade; bring to the boil. Reduce heat; simmer, uncovered, over low heat, about 2 hours or until sauce has thickened. Season.

prep + cook time 2 hours 35 minutes (+ refrigeration)
serves 4
nutritional count per serving 27.9g total fat (5.7g saturated fat); 2284kJ (546 cal); 12.8g carbohydrate; 54.3g protein; 4.6g fibre

serving suggestion Crusty bread.

note Ask the butcher to chop the rabbit into pieces for you.

This soup is our take on the classic avgolemono (which translates as egg and lemon). There are as many variations of this soup as there are Greek families, but the avgolemono mixture, added near the end of the cooking time, is always the crowning glory.

chicken, lemon and rice soup

2 teaspoons olive oil
1 small brown onion (80g), chopped finely
1 litre (4 cups) chicken stock
400g (12½ ounces) chicken breast fillets, chopped coarsely
⅓ cup (65g) arborio rice
2 eggs
⅓ cup (80ml) lemon juice
2 tablespoons finely chopped fresh flat-leaf parsley

1 Heat oil in large saucepan; cook onion, stirring, until softens. Add stock, chicken and rice; bring to the boil. Reduce heat; simmer, covered, about 20 minutes or until rice is tender. Remove from heat.
2 Whisk eggs and juice in small bowl until smooth. Gradually whisk ½ cup hot soup into egg mixture, then stir warmed egg mixture back into soup.
3 Serve bowls of soup sprinkled with parsley.

prep + cook time 45 minutes serves 4
nutritional count per serving 8.4g total fat (2.3g saturated fat); 1099kJ (263 cal); 16.3g carbohydrate; 30.3g protein; 0.5g fibre

note Arborio rice is an excellent choice for this recipe due to its high starch level, making for a deliciously creamy soup.

greek salad

¼ cup (60ml) olive oil
1 tablespoon lemon juice
1 tablespoon white wine vinegar
1 tablespoon finely chopped fresh oregano
1 clove garlic, crushed
3 medium tomatoes (450g), cut into wedges
2 lebanese cucumbers (260g), chopped coarsely
200g (6½ ounces) fetta cheese, chopped coarsely
1 small red capsicum (bell pepper) (150g),
  sliced thinly
1 small red onion (100g), sliced thinly
½ cup (75g) seeded black olives

1 Whisk oil, juice, vinegar, oregano and garlic in large bowl.
2 Add remaining ingredients to bowl; toss gently to combine.

prep time 20 minutes **serves** 4
nutritional count per serving 25.8g total fat (9.6g saturated fat); 1359kJ (325 cal); 10.8g carbohydrate; 11.5g protein; 3.2g fibre

eggplant salad

1 large eggplant (500g)

PARSLEY DRESSING
¼ cup coarsely chopped fresh flat-leaf parsley
1 clove garlic, crushed
1 teaspoon rigani
2 tablespoons olive oil
1 tablespoon lemon juice

1 Preheat oven to 200°C/400°F.
2 Place eggplant on oven tray; prick all over with a fork. Roast eggplant about 40 minutes, turning occasionally, until very soft. Cool; peel.
3 Meanwhile, make parsley dressing.
4 Tear eggplant flesh into long strips. Serve with dressing.

PARSLEY DRESSING Combine ingredients in small bowl; season to taste.

prep + cook time 50 minutes (+ cooling)
serves 4 as a side
nutritional count per serving 9.5g total fat (1.5g saturated fat); 424kJ (101 cal); 3.1g carbohydrate; 1.3g protein; 3.1g fibre

roasted garlic lemon and oregano chicken

1.5kg (3 pounds) medium potatoes,
  quartered lengthways
4 chicken marylands (1.4kg)
½ cup (125ml) lemon juice
½ cup (125ml) olive oil
6 cloves garlic, chopped finely
2 teaspoons rigani
1½ cups (375ml) water

1 Preheat oven to 180°C/350°F.
2 Place potatoes in large baking dish; top with chicken. Combine juice, oil, garlic and rigani in small jug; pour into dish. Add the water to dish; season with salt and ground white pepper.
3 Roast chicken and potatoes, uncovered, about 1½ hours or until chicken is tender and browned.

prep + cook time 1 hour 40 minutes **serves** 4
nutritional count per serving 46.2g total fat (9.8g saturated fat); 3793kJ (906 cal); 48.1g carbohydrate; 73.5g protein; 7.3g fibre

serving suggestion Green salad.

lentil soup

1 tablespoon olive oil
1 medium brown onion (150g), chopped finely
2 cloves garlic, crushed
1 cup (200g) brown lentils, rinsed, drained
400g (12½ ounces) canned diced tomatoes
1½ cups (375ml) chicken stock
1½ cups (375ml) water
1 bay leaf
2 tablespoons coarsely chopped fresh dill

1   Heat oil in large saucepan; cook onion, stirring, until softened. Stir in garlic; cook until fragrant.
2   Stir in lentils, undrained tomatoes, stock, the water and bay leaf; bring to the boil. Simmer, covered, about 50 minutes or until lentils are tender. Season to taste. Discard bay leaf. Serve sprinkled with dill.

prep + cook time 1 hour **serves** 4
nutritional count per serving 6.2g total fat (1g saturated fat); 880kJ (210 cal); 25.3g carbohydrate; 14.2g protein; 9.2g fibre

serving suggestions A dash of red wine vinegar for each bowl and crusty bread.

quail, fig and orange salad

6 quails (1.2kg)
3 medium oranges (720g)
4 medium fresh figs (240g), quartered
100g (3 ounces) mizuna
½ cup (60g) coarsely chopped roasted pecans

MAPLE ORANGE DRESSING
⅓ cup (80ml) orange juice
¼ cup (60ml) olive oil
2 tablespoons pure maple syrup
1 clove garlic, crushed

1 Make maple orange dressing.
2 Rinse quail under cold water; pat dry with absorbent paper. Discard neck from quail. Using kitchen scissors, cut along each side of quail's backbone; discard backbones. Halve quail along breastbone; brush quail halves with half the dressing.
3 Cook quail on heated oiled grill plate (or grill or barbecue) until cooked through.
4 Meanwhile, segment oranges over large bowl. Add remaining ingredients and remaining dressing to bowl; toss gently to combine.
5 Divide salad among serving plates; top with quail.

MAPLE ORANGE DRESSING Place ingredients in screw-top jar; shake well.

prep + cook time 35 minutes serves 4
nutritional count per serving 41.5g total fat (7g saturated fat); 2571kJ (615 cal); 26.8g carbohydrate; 32.3g protein; 5.9g fibre

prawn, pink grapefruit and fetta salad

24 cooked large king prawns (shrimp) (1.6kg)
1 baby cos lettuce (180g), trimmed,
 leaves separated
2 small pink grapefruits (700g), segmented
200g (6½ ounces) fetta cheese, crumbled

CHILLI MINT DRESSING
¼ cup (60ml) olive oil
¼ cup (60ml) red wine vinegar
1 teaspoon sugar
¼ cup coarsely chopped fresh mint
1 fresh long red chilli, sliced thinly

1 Shell and devein prawns, leaving tails intact.
2 Make chilli mint dressing.
3 Divide lettuce, prawns, grapefruit and cheese
among serving plates; drizzle with dressing.

CHILLI MINT DRESSING Place ingredients
in screw-top jar; shake well.

prep time 30 minutes **serves** 8
nutritional count per serving 17.9g total fat (6.5g
saturated fat); 1346kJ (322 cal); 5.1g carbohydrate;
34.5g protein; 1.2g fibre

braised borlotti beans with tomato and garlic

500g (1 pound) fresh borlotti beans, shelled
⅓ cup (80ml) olive oil
1 cup (250ml) water
1 bulb garlic, cut in half horizontally
3 large ripe tomatoes (450g), chopped coarsely
¼ cup fresh oregano leaves
½ cup coarsely chopped fresh basil

1 Preheat oven to 180°C/350°F.
2 Place beans in medium baking dish; drizzle
with oil and the water. Add garlic, tomato and
oregano; bake, covered, about 1¼ hours or until
beans are tender. Stir in basil.

prep + cook time 1 hour 25 minutes **serves** 4
nutritional count per serving 18.4g total fat (2.6g
saturated fat); 752kJ (180 cal); 2.3g carbohydrate;
1.2g protein; 1.6g fibre

moussaka

¼ cup (60ml) olive oil
2 large eggplants (1kg), sliced thinly
1 large brown onion (200g), chopped finely
2 cloves garlic, crushed
1kg (2 pounds) minced (ground) lamb
410g (13 ounces) canned crushed tomatoes
½ cup (125ml) dry white wine
1 teaspoon ground cinnamon
¼ cup (20g) finely grated kefalotyri cheese

WHITE SAUCE
75g (2½ ounces) butter
⅓ cup (50g) plain (all-purpose) flour
2 cups (500ml) milk

1 Heat oil in large frying pan; cook eggplant, in batches, until browned both sides. Drain on absorbent paper.
2 Cook onion and garlic in same pan, stirring, until onion softens. Add lamb; cook, stirring, until lamb changes colour. Stir in undrained tomatoes, wine and cinnamon; bring to the boil. Reduce heat; simmer, uncovered, about 30 minutes or until liquid has evaporated.
3 Meanwhile, preheat oven to 180°C/350°F. Oil shallow 2-litre (8-cup) rectangular baking dish.
4 Make white sauce.
5 Place one-third of the eggplant, overlapping slices slightly, in dish; spread half the meat sauce over eggplant. Repeat layering with another third of the eggplant, remaining meat sauce and remaining eggplant. Spread white sauce over top layer of eggplant; sprinkle with cheese.
6 Bake moussaka about 40 minutes or until top browns lightly. Cover; stand 10 minutes before serving.

WHITE SAUCE Melt butter in medium saucepan, add flour; cook, stirring, until mixture bubbles and thickens. Gradually add milk; stir until mixture boils and thickens.

prep + cook time 1 hour 50 minutes serves 6
nutritional count per serving 36.6g total fat (16.5g saturated fat); 2420kJ (579 cal); 18g carbohydrate; 41.8g protein; 5.3g fibre

serving suggestion Green salad.

slow-cooked potatoes with wine and herbs

1 medium lemon (140g)
600g (1¼ pounds) kipfler potatoes,
 halved lengthways
1 tablespoon olive oil
1 medium brown onion (150g), sliced thinly
12 unpeeled garlic cloves
1 tablespoon rigani
4 bay leaves
½ cup (125ml) dry white wine
1 cup (250ml) chicken stock
⅓ cup (50g) kalamata olives
⅓ cup (65g) fetta cheese, crumbled

1 Preheat oven to 160°C/325°F.
2 Finely grate rind from the lemon. Squeeze
lemon; you need ¼ cup juice. Combine potatoes
and juice in bowl; season.
3 Heat oil in medium baking dish; cook onion
and garlic, stirring, until onion softens. Add
potatoes with juice, rigani, rind and bay leaves;
stir to coat in onion mixture. Add wine and stock;
bring to the boil.
4 Roast potato mixture, uncovered, in oven,
stirring occasionally, about 40 minutes or until
potatoes are tender.
5 Serve potatoes with olives and fetta.

prep + cook time 55 minutes **serves** 4 as a side
nutritional count per serving 11g total fat (3.6g
saturated fat); 970kJ (232 cal); 22.8g carbohydrate;
8g protein; 5.3g fibre

broad beans and artichokes

300g (9½ ounces) fresh or frozen broad beans
  (fava beans)
400g (12½ ounces) canned artichokes,
  drained, halved

TOMATO DRESSING
1 medium tomato (150g), seeded, chopped finely
2 tablespoons finely shredded fresh basil leaves
2 tablespoons olive oil
1 tablespoon white wine vinegar

1 Make tomato dressing.
2 Add shelled broad beans to saucepan of boiling
salted water, boil, uncovered, about 2 minutes or
until skins wrinkle; drain. Transfer to bowl of iced
water, stand 2 minutes; drain.
3 Peel broad beans. Place beans in medium bowl
with artichokes and dressing; toss gently to
combine. Season to taste.

TOMATO DRESSING Combine ingredients in
small bowl; season to taste.

prep + cook time 20 minutes serves 4
nutritional count per serving 9.5g total fat (1.5g
saturated fat); 539kJ (129 cal); 4.4g carbohydrate;
6.1g protein; 10.6g fibre

note You will need about 1.25kg (2½ pounds)
fresh broad beans for this recipe.

grilled lemon chicken

½ cup (125ml) olive oil
½ cup (125ml) lemon juice
1.5kg (3 pounds) chicken thigh fillets
2 teaspoons rigani
2 teaspoons coarse cooking salt
1 teaspoon ground white pepper
1 medium lemon (140g), cut into wedges

1 Blend or process oil and juice until thick and creamy.
2 Combine chicken, rigani, salt, pepper and half the lemon mixture in medium bowl. Thread chicken onto eight oiled metal skewers.
3 Cook skewers on heated oiled grill plate (or grill or barbecue or grill pan), brushing frequently with remaining lemon mixture until cooked through.
4 Serve skewers with lemon wedges.

prep + cook time 30 minutes **serves** 8
nutritional count per serving 30g total fat (7g saturated fat); 1690kJ (404 cal); 1g carbohydrate; 33g protein; 0.1g fibre

serving suggestion Green salad.

lemon and garlic lamb kebabs

8 x 15cm (6-inch) stalks fresh rosemary
750g (1½ pounds) lamb fillets,
    cut into 3cm (1¼-inch) pieces
3 cloves garlic, crushed
2 tablespoons olive oil
2 teaspoons finely grated lemon rind
1 tablespoon lemon juice

1   Remove leaves from bottom two-thirds of each rosemary stalk; sharpen trimmed ends to a point.
2   Thread lamb onto rosemary skewers. Brush kebabs with combined garlic, oil, rind and juice. Cover; refrigerate until required.
3   Cook kebabs on heated oiled grill plate (or grill or barbecue), brushing frequently with remaining garlic mixture, until cooked.
4   Serve kebabs with a greek salad, if you like.

prep + cook time 30 minutes **serves** 4
nutritional count per serving 15.9g total fat (4.3g saturated fat); 1250kJ (299 cal); 0.4g carbohydrate; 38.6g protein; 0.4g fibre

roast leg of lamb with potatoes and artichokes

1.2kg (2½-pound) leg of lamb
2 cloves garlic, sliced
6 small unpeeled potatoes (720g), quartered
1 medium lemon (140g), quartered
3 sprigs fresh thyme
1½ tablespoons olive oil
400g (12½ ounces) canned artichokes in brine,
  drained

1 Preheat oven to 240°C/450°F.
2 Pierce lamb all over with small sharp knife;
press garlic into cuts.
3 Place lamb in large baking dish. Place potatoes,
lemon and thyme in single layer around lamb;
season. Rub oil over lamb and potatoes. Roast,
uncovered, 20 minutes. Reduce oven to 200°C/400°F;
roast, uncovered, about 30 minutes or until lamb is
cooked as desired. Remove lamb from dish; stand,
covered, 15 minutes.
4 Meanwhile, increase oven to 220°C/425°F. Add
artichokes to dish; roast, uncovered, 15 minutes.
5 Serve lamb sliced with potatoes and artichokes.

prep + cook time 1 hour 25 minutes serves 4
nutritional count per serving 23g total fat (7g
saturated fat); 2145kJ (512 cal); 24.4g carbohydrate;
51.8g protein; 9.7g fibre

note For this cooking time, the lamb will be pink.
If you prefer it well done, roast a further 20 minutes at 200°C/400°F.

pastitsio

250g (8 ounces) macaroni pasta
2 eggs, beaten lightly
¾ cup (60g) coarsely grated kefalotyri cheese
2 tablespoons fresh breadcrumbs

MEAT SAUCE
2 tablespoons olive oil
2 medium brown onions (300g), chopped finely
750g (1½ pounds) minced (ground) lamb
410g (13 ounces) canned crushed tomatoes
⅓ cup (90g) tomato paste
½ cup (125ml) beef stock
¼ cup (60ml) dry white wine
½ teaspoon ground cinnamon
1 egg, beaten lightly

CHEESE SAUCE
90g (3 ounces) butter
½ cup (75g) plain (all-purpose) flour
3½ cups (875ml) milk
1 cup (80g) coarsely grated kefalotyri cheese
2 egg yolks

1 Preheat oven to 180°C/350°F. Oil shallow 2.5-litre (10-cup) ovenproof dish.
2 Make meat sauce and cheese sauce.
3 Cook pasta in large saucepan of boiling water until tender; drain. Combine hot pasta, egg and cheese in large bowl. Press pasta over base of dish.
4 Top pasta evenly with meat sauce; pour over cheese sauce. Smooth surface; sprinkle with breadcrumbs.
5 Bake pastitsio about 1 hour or until browned lightly. Stand 10 minutes before serving.

MEAT SAUCE Heat oil in large saucepan; cook onion and lamb, stirring, until lamb is browned. Stir in tomato, paste, stock, wine and cinnamon; simmer, uncovered, 20 minutes or until mixture is thick. Cool; stir in egg.

CHEESE SAUCE Melt butter in medium saucepan, add flour; cook, stirring, until mixture bubbles and thickens. Remove from heat; gradually stir in milk. Stir over heat until sauce boils and thickens; stir in cheese. Cool 5 minutes; stir in egg yolks.

prep + cook time 2 hours 15 minutes serves 6
nutritional count per serving 45.8g total fat (23.2g saturated fat); 3440kJ (823 cal); 51.6g carbohydrate; 48.4g protein; 4g fibre

lamb shanks with lentils

1 tablespoon olive oil
6 french-trimmed lamb shanks (1.5kg)
1 large brown onion (200g), chopped finely
2 stalks celery (300g), trimmed, chopped finely
1 medium carrot (120g), sliced finely
2 bay leaves
3 cups (750ml) chicken stock
1 cup (250ml) water
1¼ cups (250g) brown lentils, rinsed, drained
2 tablespoons lemon juice
2 tablespoons coarsely chopped fresh
    flat-leaf parsley

1 Heat oil in large saucepan; cook lamb, in batches, until browned. Remove from pan.
2 Add onion, celery, carrot and bay leaves to pan; cook, stirring, about 5 minutes or until onion softens.
3 Return lamb to pan with stock and the water; bring to the boil. Reduce heat; simmer, covered, 1 hour. Stir in lentils; bring to the boil. Reduce heat; simmer, covered, 30 minutes. Uncover; simmer further 30 minutes or until lamb and lentils are tender.
4 Stir in juice and parsley; season to taste.

prep + cook time 2 hours 30 minutes **serves** 6
nutritional count per serving 12.1g total fat (4.3g saturated fat); 1547kJ (370 cal); 20.8g carbohydrate; 41.5g protein; 7.4g fibre

serving suggestion Wild rocket salad.

stuffed eggplant with lamb and rice

2 large eggplants (1kg), halved
¼ cup (60ml) olive oil
1 medium brown onion (150g), chopped finely
300g (9½ ounces) minced (ground) lamb
3 cloves garlic, crushed
⅓ cup (65g) medium-grain rice
½ cup (125ml) water
1 tablespoon lemon juice
2 teaspoons rigani
⅔ cup (50g) coarsely grated kefalograviera cheese

1 Preheat oven to 220°C/425°F.
2 Cut a 1cm (½-inch) border inside each
eggplant; scoop out flesh without breaking skin.
Place eggplant shells on oven tray; brush with
1 tablespoon of the oil. Roast about 20 minutes or
until tender.
3 Meanwhile, coarsely chop eggplant flesh. Heat
1 tablespoon of the oil in medium frying pan; cook
eggplant, stirring, until tender. Remove from pan.
4 Heat remaining oil in same pan; cook onion,
stirring, until softened. Add lamb; cook, stirring,
until browned. Add garlic, cook, stirring, until
fragrant. Return eggplant to pan with rice and
the water; cook, covered, over low heat, about
10 minutes or until rice is tender. Stir in juice and
rigani; season to taste.
5 Spoon lamb mixture into eggplant shells;
sprinkle with cheese. Roast about 20 minutes or
until cheese is browned.

prep + cook time 1 hour **serves** 4
nutritional count per serving 28.4g total fat (8.5g
saturated fat); 1800kJ (430 cal); 20.5g carbohydrate;
23.6g protein; 7.2g fibre

serving suggestion Greek salad.

goat and haricot bean casserole

2 cups (400g) dried haricot beans
¼ cup (60ml) olive oil
2kg (4-pound) leg of goat, boned
2 medium onions (300g), chopped finely
2 cloves garlic, crushed
2 x 425g (13½ ounces) canned crushed tomatoes
½ cup (125ml) dry red wine
¼ cup (60ml) tomato paste
1 cinnamon stick
1 tablespoon lemon juice
2 tablespoons coarsely chopped fresh parsley

1 Place beans in bowl; cover well with cold water. Stand overnight; drain.
2 Cook beans in large saucepan of boiling water; simmer, uncovered, about 30 minutes or until tender; drain well.
3 Meanwhile, coarsely chop goat. Heat oil in large saucepan; cook goat, in batches, until well browned. Remove from pan.
4 Cook onion and garlic in same pan, stirring, until onion softens. Return goat to pan with undrained tomatoes, wine, paste and cinnamon; simmer, covered, 2 hours or until goat is tender, stirring occasionally.
5 Add beans, juice and parsley; season to taste. Stir until heated through.

prep + cook time 2 hours 30 minutes (+ standing)
serves 6
nutritional count per serving 32.4g total fat (12g saturated fat); 2855kJ (683 cal); 17.8g carbohydrate; 77g protein; 7.6g fibre

note You will need to order goat from a specialist continental butcher; this casserole is equally delicious made using lamb. Ask the butcher to bone the leg for you.

goat and capsicum stew

¼ cup (60ml) olive oil
1.6kg (3¼-pound) boneless goat shoulder, chopped coarsely
2 medium brown onions (300g), sliced thinly
1 bay leaf
400g (12½ ounce) canned diced tomatoes
½ cup (125ml) chicken stock
2 teaspoons rigani
2 medium red capsicums (bell peppers) (400g), sliced thinly
1 medium yellow capsicum (bell pepper) (200g), sliced thinly
2 tablespoons coarsely chopped flat leaf parsley

1 Heat 2 tablespoons of the oil in large saucepan; cook goat, in batches, until browned. Remove from pan.
2 Heat remaining oil in same pan; cook onion and bay leaf, stirring, until onion softens. Return goat to pan with undrained tomatoes, stock and rigani; bring to the boil. Reduce heat; simmer, covered, 2½ hours.
3 Stir in capsicum; simmer, covered, 20 minutes or until capsicum is tender. Season to taste. Serve sprinkled with parsley.

prep + cook time 3 hours 15 minutes **serves** 6
nutritional count per serving 17.5g total fat (4.1g saturated fat); 2105kJ (503 cal); 6.9g carbohydrate; 74.5g protein; 3.3g fibre

serving suggestions Rice or mashed potatoes.

note Goat shoulder is good for stews and casseroles as it needs long slow cooking to be tender. It is sold in Greek and specialty butchers and often comes frozen. Ask the butcher to cut the meat into chunks while frozen and thaw meat in refrigerator at home.

rabbit with olives, parsley and pine nuts

1.4kg (2¾-pound) whole rabbit
1 cup (150g) fetta-stuffed green olives
½ cup loosely packed fresh flat-leaf parsley leaves
⅓ cup (50g) pine nuts, roasted
1½ cups (375ml) dry white wine
½ cup (125ml) water
½ cup (125ml) olive oil
2 teaspoons finely chopped fresh rosemary

1 Preheat oven to 160°C/325°F. Oil large baking dish.
2 Rinse rabbit under cold water; pat dry inside and out with absorbent paper. Place rabbit in baking dish; fill cavity of rabbit with combined olives, parsley and pine nuts. Tie at intervals with kitchen string.
3 Combine wine, the water, oil and rosemary in small jug; pour over rabbit. Season with salt and pepper.
4 Roast rabbit about 1½ hours or until rabbit is tender. Serve rabbit drizzled with pan juices.

prep + cook time 1 hour 45 minutes **serves** 4
nutritional count per serving 54.3g total fat (9g saturated fat); 3098kJ (740 cal); 2.4g carbohydrate; 53g protein; 2.1g fibre

serving suggestions Crusty bread and green salad.

goat kleftiko

1.5kg (3-pound) goat shoulder
3 cloves garlic, sliced
2 tablespoons olive oil
¼ cup coarsely chopped fresh oregano
1 tablespoon finely grated lemon rind
2 tablespoons lemon juice
90g (3 ounces) kefalograviera cheese,
   sliced thickly

1 Preheat oven to 170°C/340°F.
2 Pierce goat all over with small sharp knife, press garlic into cuts; season. Heat oil in large frying pan; cook goat until browned.
3 Layer two sheets of baking paper; fold into quarters then open. Place paper in large baking dish; place goat in centre of creases. Sprinkle goat with oregano and rind; drizzle with juice. Top with cheese; fold paper over to enclose, sealing edges to avoid juices escaping. Wrap in foil.
4 Roast goat about 2½ hours or until goat is tender. Stand 15 minutes before serving.

prep + cook time 3 hours (+ standing) serves 4
nutritional count per serving 10.5g total fat (3.6g saturated fat); 1045kJ (250 cal); 0.4g carbohydrate; 36.3g protein; 0.3g fibre

serving suggestion Pan-fried potatoes and salad.

notes Goat is sold in Greek and specialty butchers and often comes frozen. The leg of goat will give more meat than the shoulder and will take up to 4 hours to roast. The name kleftiko comes from the "klephts", bandits who used to roam the Greek countryside, stealing goats and lambs and then cooking them in a sealed pit to avoid any smoke being seen. Nowadays, the meat is cooked in a parcel or in a clay pot dish. This method ensures that all the juices and moisture remain and the meat falls off the bone.

celebrations

halva

2 cups (440g) caster (superfine) sugar
1 litre (4 cups) water
2 cloves
1 cinnamon stick
220g (7 ounces) butter, chopped coarsely
2 cups (320g) semolina
½ cup (80g) coarsely chopped blanched almonds
2 teaspoons finely grated orange rind
½ cup (80g) coarsely chopped raisins
¼ cup (40g) blanched whole almonds, roasted, extra
1 teaspoon ground cinnamon

1 Grease 20cm x 30cm (8-inch x 12-inch) slice pan or ovenproof dish; line base with baking paper, extending paper 5cm (2 inches) over short sides.
2 Stir sugar, the water, cloves and cinnamon stick in medium saucepan over heat until sugar dissolves. Bring to the boil; boil, uncovered, without stirring, 5 minutes. Cool 5 minutes.
3 Meanwhile, heat butter in large saucepan until foaming. Add semolina and chopped nuts; cook, stirring, about 8 minutes or until lightly browned. Remove from heat. Carefully strain sugar syrup into semolina mixture (mixture will bubble up).
4 Return pan to heat, add rind and raisins; cook, stirring, about 1 minute or until thick and starting to come away from the side of the pan.
5 Spread semolina mixture into pan; top with extra nuts, cool. Sprinkle with ground cinnamon before cutting.

prep + cook time 30 minutes (+ standing)
serves 20
nutritional count per serving 12.4g total fat (6g saturated fat); 1097kJ (262 cal); 36g carbohydrate; 3g protein; 1.3g fibre

easter bread (tsoureki)

6 teaspoons (21g) dry yeast
½ cup (125ml) warm water
1 cup (250ml) warm milk
1 teaspoon salt
1 teaspoon caster (superfine) sugar
155g (5 ounces) butter, softened
2 teaspoons finely grated lemon rind
1 cup (220g) caster (superfine) sugar, extra
4 eggs
6 cups (900g) plain (all-purpose) flour
2 teaspoons ground cinnamon
1 egg yolk, extra
¼ cup (20g) flaked almonds

1 Combine yeast, the water, half the milk, salt and sugar in small bowl. Cover; stand in warm place about 10 minutes or until frothy.
2 Beat butter, rind and extra sugar in small bowl with electric mixer until light and fluffy. Beat in eggs, one at a time, then remaining cooled milk (mixture will curdle at this stage, but will come together later).
3 Sift flour and cinnamon into large bowl, stir in yeast and butter mixtures; mix to a soft dough. Knead dough on floured surface about 5 minutes or until smooth and elastic. Place dough in large greased bowl. Cover; stand in warm place about 1 hour or until doubled in size.
4 Meanwhile, preheat oven to 220°C/425°F. Grease two oven trays; line with baking paper.
5 Knead dough on floured surface 2 minutes. Divide dough in half, divide each half into thirds. Roll each third into sausage-shaped lengths of about 45cm (18 inches). Plait three lengths together, shape into a ring. Repeat with remaining lengths. Place on trays; cover, stand in warm place about 30 minutes or until doubled in size.
6 Brush bread with extra egg yolk, sprinkle with nuts. Bake 20 minutes, reduce oven to 180°C/350°F; bake further 20 minutes or until browned. Cool on tray 5 minutes. Serve warm or cold.

prep + cook time 1 hour 30 minutes (+ standing)
serves 16
nutritional count per serving 10.9g total fat (5.9g saturated fat); 1496kJ (357 cal); 56.3g carbohydrate; 8.8g protein; 2.5g fibre

notes A few red-dyed, hard-boiled eggs can also be positioned at even intervals when plaiting the dough. You could also decorate the bread with sesame seeds or slivered almonds.

easter butter biscuits (koulourakia)

125g (4 ounces) butter, melted
1 teaspoon vanilla extract
2 teaspoons finely grated orange rind
⅔ cup (150g) caster (superfine) sugar
2 eggs
2 tablespoons milk
3 cups (450g) self-raising flour
1 egg yolk, extra
2 tablespoons sesame seeds
¼ cup (35g) slivered almonds

1 Preheat oven to 180°C/350°F. Grease oven trays; line with baking paper.
2 Beat butter, extract, rind and sugar in small bowl with electric mixer until combined. Beat in eggs, one at a time; do not over-beat. Transfer mixture to large bowl; stir in milk and sifted flour, in two batches. Turn dough onto floured surface; knead lightly until smooth.
3 Divide dough into 10 balls; divide each ball into five balls. Roll each ball into 15cm (6-inch) sausage-shaped lengths, then cut into 10cm (4-inch) lengths. Shape lengths into scrolls, twists and figure eights; place about 2.5cm (1 inch) apart on trays. Brush with extra egg yolk, sprinkle with seeds and nuts.
4 Bake biscuits about 15 minutes; cool on trays.

prep + cook time 1 hour **makes** 50
nutritional count per biscuit 3g total fat (1.5g saturated fat); 300kJ (72 cal); 9.6g carbohydrate; 1.6g protein; 0.5g fibre

moist carrot and apple cake

2 cups (300g) self-raising flour
1 teaspoon bicarbonate of soda (baking soda)
1 cup (220g) caster (superfine) sugar
4 cups (960g) coarsely grated carrot
2 cups (340g) coarsely grated apple
1 tablespoon finely grated orange rind
¼ cup (60ml) orange juice
¾ cup (180ml) olive oil
⅓ cup (80ml) brandy
1 cup (150g) roasted pine nuts
2 teaspoons icing (confectioners') sugar

1   Preheat oven to 180°C/350°F. Grease 25cm
(10-inch) springform tin; line base and side with
baking paper.
2   Sift flour and soda into large bowl; stir in caster
sugar, carrot, apple and rind. Stir in juice, oil,
brandy and pine nuts. Pour mixture into pan.
3   Bake cake about 1 hour. Stand cake 10 minutes
before removing from springform tin. Serve dusted
with sifted icing sugar.

prep + cook time 1 hour 20 minutes (+ standing)
serves 12
nutritional count per serving 22.8g total fat (2.8g
saturated fat); 1720kJ (410 cal); 44.5g carbohydrate;
5g protein; 5.3g fibre

easter cheese pies (flaounes)

2 teaspoons (7g) dry yeast
1 cup (250ml) warm water
1 cup (250ml) warm milk
1 teaspoon salt
2 teaspoons caster (superfine) sugar
5 cups (750g) plain (all-purpose) flour
2 tablespoons olive oil
40g (1½ ounces) butter, melted
1 egg, beaten lightly
¼ cup (35g) sesame seeds

CHEESE FILLING
2 cups (250g) coarsely grated kasseri cheese
1⅓ cups (180g) coarsely grated haloumi cheese
1 tablespoon semolina
2 tablespoons finely chopped fresh mint
4 eggs

1 Combine yeast, the water, milk, salt and sugar in small bowl. Cover; stand in warm place about 10 minutes or until frothy.
2 Sift flour into large bowl, stir in yeast mixture, then oil and butter, mix to soft dough. Knead dough on floured surface about 5 minutes or until smooth and elastic. Place dough in large oiled bowl, turn to coat. Cover; stand in warm place about 1 hour or until doubled in size.
3 Meanwhile, preheat oven to 220°C/425°F. Oil four oven trays; line with baking paper.
4 Make cheese filling.
5 Knead dough on floured surface 2 minutes. Working with half the dough at a time, roll dough to 5mm (¼-inch) thick; cut out 10.5cm (4¼-inch) rounds. Drop level tablespoons of filling into centre of each round; brush edge with egg. Shape into a triangle by folding over three sides; pinch edges together, leaving a little filling exposed. Place on trays 3cm (1¼ inches) apart; brush with more egg, sprinkle with seeds.
6 Bake flaounes about 15 minutes or until browned and puffed. Serve warm or cold.

CHEESE FILLING Combine ingredients in medium bowl; season.

prep + cook time 1 hour (+ standing) makes 32
nutritional count per pastry 6.8g total fat (3.1g saturated fat); 686kJ (164 cal); 18.3g carbohydrate; 7.4g protein; 1g fibre

sweets

baklava

1½ cups (200g) shelled unsalted pistachio nuts
2 cups (200g) walnut pieces
¼ cup (55g) caster (superfine) sugar
2 tablespoons fine semolina
1 teaspoon ground cinnamon
pinch ground cloves
375g (12 ounces) fillo pastry
310g (10 ounces) butter, melted
30 whole cloves

SYRUP
1 cup (220g) caster (superfine) sugar
1 cup (250ml) water
¼ cup (90g) honey
1 tablespoon lemon juice
1 cinnamon stick

1 Preheat oven to 200°C/400°F. Grease 20cm x 30cm (8-inch x 12-inch) lamington pan.
2 Process nuts, sugar, semolina, cinnamon and ground cloves until chopped finely; transfer to medium bowl.

3 Brush 1 sheet of pastry with a little of the butter; top with 7 more sheets, brushing each well with butter. Fold pastry in half, place into pan. Sprinkle pastry with thin even layer of the nut mixture. Layer another 2 sheets of pastry, brushing each well with more butter. Fold pastry in half, place in pan; top with another layer of nut mixture. Repeat layering process until all nut mixture has been used. Repeat layering and buttering with any remaining pastry sheets; brush the final layer with butter. Score the top lightly in diamond pattern; press one whole clove into centre of each piece.
4 Bake baklava about 50 minutes.
5 Meanwhile, make syrup.
6 Pour syrup over hot baklava. Cool before cutting.

SYRUP Stir ingredients in small saucepan over heat until sugar dissolves; bring to the boil. Reduce heat; simmer, uncovered, about 10 minutes or until thickened slightly. Discard cinnamon; cool syrup.

prep + cook time 1 hour 20 minutes (+ cooling)
makes 30
nutritional count per piece 16.4g total fat (6.1g saturated fat); 1010kJ (240 cal); 21g carbohydrate; 3.6g protein; 1.4g fibre

note When working with the first eight sheets of pastry, cover remaining pastry with a sheet of baking paper then a damp tea towel to prevent it from drying out.

honey walnut biscuits

1 cup (250ml) vegetable oil
½ cup (110g) caster (superfine) sugar
½ cup (125ml) orange juice
2 tablespoons brandy
1 egg
4 cups (600g) self-raising flour
1 cup (160g) fine semolina
1 teaspoon ground cinnamon
1 cup (100g) walnut pieces, chopped finely

SPICED SYRUP
1 cup (220g) caster (superfine) sugar
½ cup (175g) honey
½ cup (125ml) water
2 tablespoons lemon juice
1 cinnamon stick
6 cloves

1 Preheat oven to 160°C/325°F. Grease oven trays; line with baking paper.
2 Combine oil, sugar, juice, brandy and egg in large bowl. Stir in sifted flour, semolina and half the cinnamon.
3 Roll level tablespoons of mixture into 6cm (2½-inch) oval shapes. Place on trays, about 4cm (1½ inches) apart.
4 Bake biscuits about 25 minutes. Cool on trays.
5 Meanwhile, make spiced syrup.
6 Dip biscuits, in batches, into hot syrup for about 30 seconds or until well coated; transfer to wire rack. Sprinkle biscuits with combined walnuts and remaining cinnamon. Cool.

SPICED SYRUP Stir ingredients in small saucepan over heat until sugar dissolves; bring to the boil. Reduce heat; simmer, uncovered, about 7 minutes or until thickened slightly. Strain syrup into heatproof bowl.

prep + cook time 55 minutes (+ cooling) makes 48 nutritional count per biscuit 15.8g total fat (1.8g saturated fat); 1545kJ (370 cal); 51.8g carbohydrate; 5.2g protein; 1.8g fibre

milopita

3 medium apples (450g), peeled, cored, quartered
¼ cup (60ml) lemon juice
60g (2 ounces) butter
¼ cup (55g) firmly packed light brown sugar
1 teaspoon ground cinnamon
125g (4 ounces) butter, softened, extra
1 cup (220g) caster (superfine) sugar
1 tablespoon finely grated lemon rind
1 teaspoon vanilla extract
2 eggs, separated
1 cup (150g) self-raising flour
¼ cup (60ml) milk
1 tablespoon icing (confectioners') sugar

BRANDY YOGURT
1½ tablespoons brandy
3 teaspoons light brown sugar
1 cup (280g) greek-style yogurt

1 Preheat oven to 160°C/325°F. Grease 24cm (9½-inch) fluted pie dish.
2 Slice apple thinly; combine in medium bowl with juice. Stir butter, brown sugar and cinnamon in small saucepan over heat until sugar dissolves.
3 Beat extra butter, caster sugar, rind, extract and egg yolks in small bowl with electric mixer until light and fluffy. Stir in sifted flour and milk, in two batches.
4 Beat egg whites in small bowl with electric mixer until soft peaks form; fold into cake mixture, in two batches. Spread mixture into dish.
5 Drain apples; discard juice, return apples to bowl. Stir warm brown sugar mixture into apples. Arrange apple slices over batter in dish; drizzle with brown sugar mixture. Bake about 45 minutes.
6 Meanwhile, make brandy yogurt.
7 Dust milopita with sifted icing sugar; serve warm with brandy yogurt.

BRANDY YOGURT Stir brandy and sugar in small bowl until sugar dissolves; stir in yogurt.

prep + cook time 1 hour 30 minutes serves 8
nutritional count per serving 22.5g total fat (14.2g saturated fat); 1962kJ (470 cal); 61.1g carbohydrate; 6.2g protein; 1.8g fibre

greek coffee

1 cup (250ml) cold water
1½ tablespoons ground greek coffee
3 teaspoons caster (superfine) sugar

1 Place the water in 4 demitasse-cup capacity briki or small saucepan. Add coffee and sugar; stir over low heat until sugar dissolves. Slowly bring to the boil; remove from heat when froth almost reaches the top of briki.
2 Divide froth among 4 demitasse cups, then carefully fill the cups with remaining coffee mixture.
3 Serve coffee immediately with a glass of cold water.

prep + cook time 10 minutes **serves** 4
nutritional count per serving 0g total fat (0g saturated fat); 107kJ (26 cal); 6g carbohydrate; 0.6g protein; 0.7g fibre

note A traditional briki (small pot) is the best pot to use when making Greek coffee because it allows the proper amount of froth to form which in turn adds to the unique taste. Brikis are available from Greek and Middle Eastern delicatessens. A demitasse cup holds about ¼ cup (60ml).

rice pudding with cinnamon and vanilla bean

3 cups (750ml) milk
¼ cup (55g) caster (superfine) sugar
2 x 5cm (2-inch) strips lemon rind
1 vanilla bean, split lengthways
1 cinnamon stick
⅓ cup (65g) white medium-grain rice
3 egg yolks
⅓ cup (35g) walnuts, roasted, chopped coarsely
¼ teaspoon ground cinnamon

1 Combine milk, sugar and rind in medium saucepan; bring to the boil, stirring occasionally. Add vanilla bean and cinnamon stick, gradually stir in rice; cook, covered tightly, over low heat, stirring occasionally, about 40 minutes or until rice is tender. Discard rind, cinnamon stick and vanilla bean.
2 Combine 1 tablespoon of the hot milk mixture with egg yolks in small heatproof jug. Pour egg yolk mixture into rice, stirring over low heat, until mixture thickens.
3 Serve pudding sprinkled with nuts and ground cinnamon.

prep + cook time 55 minutes **serves** 4
nutritional count per serving 11.6g total fat (5.6g saturated fat); 1282kJ (306 cal); 42g carbohydrate; 9.8g protein; 0.4g fibre

note This dish can be served warm or at room temperature.

note Serve when guests arrive at your house with a glass of cold water.

cherry spoon sweet

425g (13½ ounces) canned seedless
  black cherries in syrup
1 cup (220g) caster (superfine) sugar
1 vanilla bean, split lengthways
2 x 5cm (2-inch) strips lemon rind
1 teaspoon lemon juice

1 Drain cherries over small saucepan; reserve cherries.
2 Add sugar, vanilla bean, rind and juice to pan; stir over heat until sugar dissolves.
3 Add reserved cherries, bring to the boil; boil, uncovered, about 7 minutes or until mixture thickens and will coat the back of a metal spoon. Cool to room temperature.

prep + cook time 15 minutes (+ cooling) serves 6
nutritional count per serving 0.1g total fat (0g saturated fat); 800kJ (191 cal); 48.7g carbohydrate; 0.6g protein; 0.7g fibre

note Myzithra cheese is the traditional Greek cheese used in this cheesecake; you could use mascarpone as a substitute.

cheesecake with brandied muscatels

125g (4 ounces) sponge finger biscuits
50g (1½ ounces) unsalted butter, melted
500g (1 pound) unsalted fresh myzithra cheese
½ cup (80g) icing (confectioners') sugar
1 tablespoon finely grated lemon rind
1 tablespoon cornflour (cornstarch)
4 eggs
½ cup (125ml) thickened (heavy) cream
2 tablespoons flaked almonds, chopped coarsely

BRANDIED MUSCATELS
¾ cup (165g) firmly packed light brown sugar
¼ cup (60ml) water
¼ cup (60ml) brandy
1 tablespoon honey
12 small clusters muscatels

1 Preheat oven to 140°C/280°F. Grease 20cm (8-inch) round springform tin; line base and side with baking paper.
2 Process biscuits until fine. Add butter, process until combined. Press mixture firmly over base of tin. Refrigerate 30 minutes.
3 Meanwhile, beat cheese, sifted icing sugar, rind and cornflour in small bowl with electric mixer until smooth. Beat in eggs, one at a time; beat in cream, in two batches. Pour mixture into tin; sprinkle with nuts.
4 Bake cheesecake about 1 hour 10 minutes. Turn oven off; leave to cool completely in oven with door ajar. Cover; refrigerate 1 hour.
5 Meanwhile, make brandied muscatels.
6 Serve cheesecake topped with muscatels and drizzled with syrup.

BRANDIED MUSCATELS Stir sugar, the water, brandy and honey in small saucepan over heat until sugar dissolves; bring to the boil. Reduce heat; simmer, uncovered, without stirring, about 5 minutes or until thickened slightly. Add muscatels; cool.

prep + cook time 1 hour 40 minutes (+ cooling & refrigeration) **serves** 12
nutritional count per serving 29.4g total fat (17.6g saturated fat); 1775kJ (424 cal); 34.5g carbohydrate; 5.1g protein; 0.5g fibre

glossary

ALLSPICE also known as pimento or jamaican pepper; tastes like a combination of nutmeg, cumin, clove and cinnamon. Available whole or ground from most supermarkets.

ALMONDS
blanched almonds with brown skins removed.
flaked paper-thin slices.
ground also known as almond meal.
slivered small pieces cut lengthways.

ARTICHOKE
globe large flower-bud of a member of the thistle family; it has tough petal-like leaves, and is edible in part when cooked.
hearts tender centre of the globe artichoke; is harvested from the plant after the prickly choke is removed. Cooked hearts can be bought from delis or canned in brine.

BAHARAT also called lebanese seven-spice; an aromatic spice blend. It is available from Middle Eastern food stores, some delis and specialist food stores.

BAKING PAPER also called parchment paper or baking parchment; a silicone-coated paper primarily used for lining baking pans and oven trays so cakes and biscuits won't stick.

BAY LEAVES aromatic leaves from the bay tree available fresh or dried; adds a strong, slightly peppery flavour.

BEANS
broad (fava) available dried, fresh, canned and frozen. Peel fresh beans twice – the outer green pod and beige-green inner shell.
lima large, flat kidney-shaped, beige dried and canned beans. Also known as butter beans.

BEETROOT (BEETS) firm, round root vegetable.

BICARBONATE OF SODA also called baking soda.

BREADCRUMBS
packaged prepared fine-textured, crunchy white breadcrumbs; good for coating foods that are to be fried.
stale made by grating, blending or processing 1- or 2-day-old bread.

BROCCOLINI a cross between broccoli and chinese kale; long asparagus-like stems with a long loose floret, both completely edible. Resembles broccoli but is milder and sweeter in taste.

BURGHUL also called bulghur wheat; hulled steamed wheat kernels that, once dried, are crushed into various sized grains. Used in Middle Eastern dishes such as felafel and tabbouleh. Is not the same as cracked wheat.

BUTTER we use salted butter; 125g is equal to 1 stick (4 ounces).

BUTTERMILK originally the term given to the slightly sour liquid left after butter was churned from cream, today it is commercially made similarly to yogurt. Sold alongside fresh milk products in supermarkets. Despite the implication of its name, it is low in fat.

CAPSICUM also called bell pepper.

CARDAMOM a spice native to India; can be purchased in pod, seed or ground form. Has a distinctive aromatic, sweetly rich flavour.

CHEESE
fetta Greek in origin; a crumbly textured goat's- or sheep-milk cheese with a sharp, salty taste. Good in salads.
haloumi a firm, traditionally sheep-milk cheese with a minty, salty flavour; holds its shape when cooked and should be eaten while still warm as it becomes tough and rubbery on cooling. Haloumi is a Cypriot cheese but is often used in Greek cooking.
kasseri a medium hard, mild flavoured sheep-milk cheese. It's stringy, rather than crumbly and is great for sandwiches or baking. Can be replaced with provolone.
kefalograviera a hard, salty, sheep or cow's-milk cheese. Its flavour is milder than kefalotyri. Can be replaced with pecorino.
kefalotyri a hard, salty cheese made from sheep and/or goat's milk. Its colour varies from white to yellow depending on the mixture of milk used in the process and its age. Great for grating over pasta or salads. Can be replaced with parmesan.

myzithra (fresh) an unsalted, soft Greek whey cheese with a mild flavour, similar to ricotta and farmer's cheese. Other varieties are also available: sour (made with goat's or sheep milk, yeast and salt) and aged (hard and salty).
parmesan also called parmigiano; is a hard, grainy cow's-milk cheese.
ricotta a soft, sweet, moist, white cow-milk cheese with a low fat content and a slightly grainy texture. Its name roughly translates as "cooked again" and refers to ricotta's manufacture from a whey that is itself a by-product of other cheese making.

CHICKEN
drumstick leg; skin and bone intact.
maryland leg and thigh connected in a single piece; bones and skin intact.
small chicken also called spatchcock or poussin; no more than 6 weeks old, weighing a maximum of 500g. Also a term to describe splitting a small chicken open, flattening then grilling.
thigh cutlet thigh with skin and centre bone intact; sometimes found skinned with bone intact.

CHICKPEAS (GARBANZO BEANS) also known as hummus or channa; an irregularly round, sandy-coloured legume. It has a firm texture even after cooking, a floury mouth-feel and robust nutty flavour; available canned or dried (reconstitute for several hours in cold water before use).

CHILLI use rubber gloves when seeding and chopping fresh chillies as they can burn your skin. We use unseeded chillies because the seeds contain the heat; use fewer chillies rather than seeding the lot.

CHOCOLATE, DARK EATING (SEMI-SWEET) also known as luxury chocolate; made of a high percentage of cocoa liquor and cocoa butter, and a little added sugar.

CINNAMON available in pieces (sticks or quills) and ground; one of the world's most common spices.

CORNICHONS French for gherkin, a very small variety of cucumber. When pickled, they are the traditional accompaniment to pâté.

CREAM, POURING we use fresh cream, also called pure cream.

CUCUMBER, LEBANESE short, slender and thin-skinned cucumber. Has tender, edible skin, tiny, yielding seeds, and sweet, fresh and flavoursome taste.

DRIED CURRANTS tiny, almost black raisins so-named after a grape variety that originated in Corinth, Greece. These are not the same as fresh currants, which are the fruit of a plant in the gooseberry family.

EGGPLANT vegetable also called aubergine.

EGGS if a recipe calls for raw or barely cooked eggs, exercise caution if there is a salmonella problem in your area, particularly in food eaten by children and pregnant women.

FENNEL BULB also called finocchio or anise; a crunchy green vegetable slightly resembling celery. Is eaten raw, fried or used as an ingredient.

FILLO PASTRY paper-thin sheets of raw pastry; brush each sheet with oil or melted butter, stack in layers, then cut and fold as directed.

FLOUR
plain also known as all-purpose.
self-raising plain or wholemeal flour with baking powder and salt added; make at home in the ratio of 1 cup flour to 2 teaspoons baking powder.
wholemeal also called wholewheat.

HARISSA a North African paste made from dried red chillies, garlic, olive oil and caraway seeds; can be used as a rub for meat, an ingredient in sauces and dressings, or eaten as a condiment. It is available from Middle Eastern food shops and some supermarkets.

HONEY the variety sold in a squeezable container is not suitable for recipes in this book.

KUMARA (ORANGE SWEET POTATO) the Polynesian name of orange-fleshed sweet potato often confused with yam; good baked, boiled, mashed or fried similarly to other potatoes.

LAMB SHANKS forequarter leg; sometimes sold as drumsticks or frenched shanks if the gristle and narrow end of the bone are discarded and the remaining meat trimmed.

LENTILS (red, brown, yellow) dried pulses often identified by and named after their colour.

MAPLE-FLAVOURED SYRUP is made from sugar cane and is also called golden or pancake syrup. It is not a substitute for pure maple syrup.

MAPLE SYRUP, PURE thin syrup distilled from the sap of the maple tree. Maple-flavoured syrup or pancake syrup is not an adequate substitute for the real thing.

MESCLUN pronounced mess-kluhn; also called mixed greens or spring salad mix. A commercial blend of assorted young lettuce and other green leaves, including baby spinach leaves, mizuna and curly endive.

MILK we use full-cream homogenised milk unless stated otherwise.

MIZUNA Japanese in origin; these frizzy green salad leaves have a delicate mustard flavour.

MUSHROOMS
button small, cultivated white mushrooms with a mild flavour.
portobello are mature, fully opened swiss browns; they are larger and bigger in flavour.
swiss brown also called roman or cremini. Light to dark brown in colour with full-bodied flavour.

NUTMEG a strong and pungent spice. Usually purchased ground, the flavour is more intense freshly grated from the whole nut (available from spice shops).

OIL
cooking-spray we use a cholesterol-free spray made from canola oil.
olive pressed from ripened olives. Extra virgin and virgin are the first and second press, respectively, and are considered the best; "extra light" or "light" on other types refers to taste not fat levels.

peanut pressed from ground peanuts; the most commonly used oil in Asian cooking because of its capacity to handle high heat without burning.
vegetable from plant rather than animal fats.

OKRA also called bamia or lady fingers. A green, ridged, oblong pod with a furry skin. Native to Africa, this vegetable can be eaten on its own; as part of a casserole, curry or gumbo; used to thicken stews or gravies.

OLIVES, KALAMATA large black olives; firm fleshed and meaty in flavour. Are preserved in vinegar or olive oil, whole or seeded.

ONION
green (scallion) also called, incorrectly, shallot; an immature onion picked before the bulb has formed, has a long, bright-green edible stalk.
red also called spanish, red spanish or bermuda onion; a sweet-flavoured, large, purple-red onion.
spring crisp, narrow green-leafed tops and a round sweet white bulb larger than green onions.

ORZO a small rice-sized pasta; similar to another small pasta, risoni.

OUZO an anise-flavoured Greek spirit.

PANCETTA an Italian unsmoked bacon. Used, sliced or chopped as an ingredient rather than eaten on its own.

PINE NUTS also called pignoli; not a nut but a small, cream-coloured kernel from pine cones. They are best roasted before use to bring out the flavour.

POLENTA also called cornmeal; a flour-like cereal made of dried corn (maize). Also the dish made from it.

POTATOES
desiree oval, smooth and pink-skinned, waxy yellow flesh; good boiled, roasted and in salads.
kipfler small, finger-shaped, nutty flavour; good baked and in salads.
lasoda round, red skin with deep eyes, white flesh; good for mashing or roasting.
sebago white skin, oval; good fried, mashed and baked.

PROSCIUTTO a kind of unsmoked Italian ham; salted, air-cured and aged, it is usually eaten uncooked.

QUAIL a small, delicate-flavoured farmed game bird related to the pheasant and partridge; it ranges in size from 250g to 300g.

RADICCHIO a red-leafed Italian chicory with a refreshing bitter taste; eaten raw and cooked.

RICE

arborio small, round grain rice well-suited to absorb a large amount of liquid; the high level of starch makes it suitable for risottos.

basmati a white, fragrant long-grained rice; the grains fluff up when cooked. It should be washed several times before cooking.

wild not a member of the rice family but the seed of an aquatic grass. Wild rice has a strong nutty taste and is often combined with brown and white rices.

RIGANI dried Greek oregano, often sold in bunches.

RISONI small rice-shape pasta; similar to another small pasta, orzo.

ROASTING/TOASTING spread nuts and dried coconut evenly on oven tray; roast in moderate oven about 5 minutes. Stir desiccated coconut, pine nuts and sesame seeds over low heat in heavy-based frying pan to toast more evenly.

ROSEWATER extract made from crushed rose petals, called gulab in India; used for its aromatic quality in many sweetmeats and desserts.

SAFFRON the stigma of a member of the crocus family, available ground or in strands; imparts a yellow-orange colour to food once infused. The quality can vary greatly; the best is the world's most expensive spice.

SEAFOOD

mussels should only be bought from a reliable fish market: they must be tightly closed when bought, indicating they are alive. Before cooking, scrub shells with a strong brush and remove the beards; do not eat any that do not open after cooking.

octopus are usually tenderised before you buy them; both octopus and squid require either long slow cooking (usually for large molluscs) or quick cooking over high heat (usually for small molluscs) – anything in between will make the octopus tough and rubbery.

prawns (shrimp) can be purchased cooked or uncooked (green), with or without shells.

squid also called calamari; a type of mollusc. Buy squid hoods to make preparation and cooking faster.

white fish fillets fillets from non-oily fish; includes bream, whiting, ling, flathead, snapper, dhufish and redfish.

SEMOLINA coarsely ground flour milled from durum wheat; flour used in making gnocchi, pasta and couscous.

SHALLOTS also called french shallots, golden shallots or eschalots. Small and elongated, with a brown-skin, they grow in tight clusters similar to garlic.

SILVER BEET (SWISS CHARD) also called, incorrectly, spinach; has fleshy stalks and large leaves, both of which can be prepared as for spinach.

SPINACH also called english spinach and, incorrectly, silver beet.

SPLIT PEAS yellow or green varieties, both with a sweet, strong pea flavour. They are usually pre-soaked but may be cooked without soaking.

SUGAR

brown a soft, finely granulated sugar retaining molasses for its colour and flavour.

caster also called superfine or finely granulated table sugar.

TAHINI a sesame seed paste; available from health food stores and the health food section in most supermarkets.

TOMATO

bottled pasta sauce a prepared sauce; a blend of tomatoes, herbs and spices.

egg (plum) also called roma, these are smallish, oval-shaped tomatoes much used in Italian cooking or salads.

paste triple-concentrated tomato puree used to flavour soups, stews and sauces.

puree canned pureed tomatoes (not tomato paste).

sun-dried tomato pieces that have been dried with salt; this dehydrates the tomato and concentrates the flavour. We use sun-dried tomatoes in oil, unless stated otherwise.

truss small vine-ripened tomatoes with vine still attached.

VANILLA

bean dried, long, thin pod; the minuscule black seeds inside are used to impart a vanilla flavour in baking and desserts.

extract obtained from vanilla beans infused in water; a non-alcoholic version of essence.

VINE LEAVES preserved grape leaves are packed in brine so rinse and dry before use. Soften fresh leaves in boiling water until pliable then dry.

VINEGAR

balsamic originally from Modena, Italy, there are now many balsamic vinegars on the market ranging in pungency and quality. Quality can be determined up to a point by price; use the most expensive sparingly.

cider made from fermented apples.

WATERCRESS one of the cress family, a large group of peppery greens used raw in salads, dips and sandwiches, or cooked in soups. Highly perishable, so it must be used as soon as possible after purchase.

WITLOF (BELGIAN ENDIVE) related to and confused with chicory. A versatile vegetable, it can be eaten cooked or raw. It is grown in darkness to prevent it becoming green; looks like a tightly furled, cream to very light-green cigar.

YEAST (dried and fresh), a raising agent. Granular (7g sachets) and fresh compressed (20g blocks) yeast can usually be substituted for each other.

YOGURT we use plain full-cream yogurt, unless stated otherwise.

ZUCCHINI also called courgette.

conversion chart

MEASURES

One Australian metric measuring cup holds approximately 250ml; one Australian metric tablespoon holds 20ml; one Australian metric teaspoon holds 5ml.

The difference between one country's measuring cups and another's is within a two- or three-teaspoon variance, and will not affect your cooking results. North America, New Zealand and the United Kingdom use a 15ml tablespoon.

All cup and spoon measurements are level. The most accurate way of measuring dry ingredients is to weigh them. When measuring liquids, use a clear glass or plastic jug with the metric markings.

We use large eggs with an average weight of 60g.

DRY MEASURES

METRIC	IMPERIAL
15g	½oz
30g	1oz
60g	2oz
90g	3oz
125g	4oz (¼lb)
155g	5oz
185g	6oz
220g	7oz
250g	8oz (½lb)
280g	9oz
315g	10oz
345g	11oz
375g	12oz (¾lb)
410g	13oz
440g	14oz
470g	15oz
500g	16oz (1lb)
750g	24oz (1½lb)
1kg	32oz (2lb)

LIQUID MEASURES

METRIC	IMPERIAL
30ml	1 fluid oz
60ml	2 fluid oz
100ml	3 fluid oz
125ml	4 fluid oz
150ml	5 fluid oz (¼ pint)
190ml	6 fluid oz
250ml	8 fluid oz
300ml	10 fluid oz (½ pint)
500ml	16 fluid oz
600ml	20 fluid oz (1 pint)
1000ml (1 litre)	1¾ pints

LENGTH MEASURES

METRIC	IMPERIAL
3mm	⅛in
6mm	¼in
1cm	½in
2cm	¾in
2.5cm	1in
5cm	2in
6cm	2½in
8cm	3in
10cm	4in
13cm	5in
15cm	6in
18cm	7in
20cm	8in
23cm	9in
25cm	10in
28cm	11in
30cm	12in (1ft)

OVEN TEMPERATURES

The oven temperatures in this book are for conventional ovens; if you have a fan-forced oven, decrease the temperature by 10-20 degrees.

	°C (CELSIUS)	°F (FAHRENHEIT)
Very slow	120	250
Slow	150	300
Moderately slow	160	325
Moderate	180	350
Moderately hot	200	400
Hot	220	425
Very hot	240	475

The imperial measurements used in these recipes are approximate only.

Measurements for cake pans are approximate only. Using same-shaped cake pans of a similar size should not affect the outcome of your baking. We measure the inside top of the cake pan to determine sizes.

index

First published in 2011 by ACP Magazines Ltd,

a division of PBL Media Pty Limited

54 Park St, Sydney

GPO Box 4088, Sydney, NSW 2001.

phone (02) 9282 8618; fax (02) 9267 9438

acpbooks@acpmagazines.com.au; www.acpbooks.com.au

ACP BOOKS

General Manager - Christine Whiston

Associate publisher - Seymour Cohen

Editor-in-Chief - Susan Tomnay

Creative Director - Hieu Chi Nguyen

Food Director - Pamela Clark

Published and Distributed in the United Kingdom by Octopus Publishing Group

Endeavour House

189 Shaftesbury Avenue

London WC2H 8JY

United Kingdom

phone (+44)(0)207 632 5400; fax (+44)(0)207 632 5405

info@octopus-publishing.co.uk;

www.octopusbooks.co.uk

Printed by Toppan Printing Co., China

International foreign language rights, Brian Cearnes, ACP Books bcearnes@acpmagazines.com.au

A catalogue record for this book is available from the British Library.

ISBN 978-1-74245-057-5

© ACP Magazines Ltd 2011

ABN 18 053 273 546